KINGS AND QUEENS
of England and Great Britain

Arms of Henry VIII
(later version)

Kings and Queens

OF ENGLAND AND
GREAT BRITAIN

Devised and Edited by

ERIC R. DELDERFIELD

Parts One and Three written
by D. V. Cook

DAVID & CHARLES

This book had its origin in three Brief Guides, devised and compiled by Eric Delderfield—one also written by Mr Delderfield and two written by D. V. Cook. Later the three were rewritten and substantially extended to form the present volume, first published in 1966.

Second edition first published 1970
Second impression 1971
Third impression 1972
Fourth impression 1973
Fifth impression 1975
Sixth impression 1977
Seventh impression 1979

Published in Great Britain by
David & Charles (Publishers) Ltd
Newton Abbot, Devon

ISBN 0 7153 5031 5 (paperback)
       0 7153 5021 8 (hardback)

Printed photolitho in Great Britain by
A. Wheaton & Co. Ltd
Exeter and London

Contents

Alphabetical Index of Plates

Illustrations in Text

COATS OF ARMS

GENEALOGICAL TREES

Acknowledgements

The plates on pages 17, 83, 118, 119, 120, 138 and 139 come from the *Radio Times* Hulton Picture Library.

All other plates are used by permission of the National Portrait Gallery, London.

Foreword

THIS book contrives to put into very brief form the principal dates, happenings and accomplishments of the reigns of all the monarchs of England from the Saxons to the present queen. No attempt has been made to give anything but the broadest possible opinion, for on the main events of history two people rarely agree. History books are invariably coloured by the opinions held by the writer but every effort has been made to avoid this in the following pages. We have endeavoured to set out the material in easy form for quick reference and at the same time to make it interesting.

Looking back, some of our kings would appear to have been callous, blood-thirsty, even criminal; undoubtedly a few were, but each age must be looked at in perspective, and the actions of the rulers—and indeed the people—must be judged by the standard of their times. The careless abandon with which Henry VIII disposed of his wives might seem atrocious unless we are prepared to give him credit for a sincere anxiety about an heir to the throne for the ultimate good of the realm. Elizabeth is often accused of callousness over the execution of Mary Queen of Scots, but the religious fanatics of the period left no doubt that there was room for only one of them. Among these rulers there were some really great by any standard of any age.

The history of this country has been a long story of religious intolerance, which has been evidenced in all reigns covered by this book. Even in the twentieth century, though blood is not shed to the same degree, we are not entirely free from this same intolerance, extending indeed well beyond religious matters.

Authentic portraits of all the earlier kings do not exist, but those which appear in this book are generally accepted as being genuine. One illustration has of necessity been taken from an effigy.

Royal corpses were often dismembered because of the desire to catch prayers for the departed soul in as many places as possible : e.g. Richard I's body was buried at Fontevrault, and his bowels at Chaluz. John's body was interred at Worcester between two Saxon saints; his heart in a gold cup at Fontevrault. When more than one place is given for 'buried' in the text it is not because there is doubt, but because the king was re-interred. Burial places cited are those where the body reposes.

Finally, in a précis of a whole reign much has to be omitted and the remainder ruthlessly compressed. We only hope that the basic facts given are clear and useful.

E. R. D.

Part One
Saxons   Normans
Plantagenets

GENEALOGY: SAXONS—PLANTAGENETS

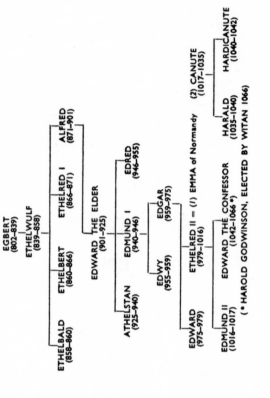

SAXONS

EGBERT
(802–839)

ETHELWULF
(839–858)

ETHELBALD
(858–860)

ETHELBERT
(860–866)

ETHELRED I
(866–871)

ALFRED
(871–901)

EDWARD THE ELDER
(901–925)

ATHELSTAN
(925–940)

EDMUND I
(940–946)

EDRED
(946–955)

EDWY
(955–959)

EDGAR
(959–975)

EDWARD
(975–979)

ETHELRED II = (1) EMMA of Normandy = (2) CANUTE
(979–1016)   (1017–1035)

EDMUND II
(1016–1017)

EDWARD THE CONFESSOR
(1042–1066 *)

HARALD
(1035–1040)

HARDICANUTE
(1040–1042)

(* HAROLD GODWINSON, ELECTED BY WITAN 1066)

NORMANS

WILLIAM I
(1066–1087)

ROBERT   WILLIAM II   HENRY I   ADELA

The dynasties

THERE have been about sixty-six monarchs of England spread over a period of about 1,150 years. These men and women have represented the following dynasties:

Saxons*.	Tudors
Normans	Stuarts
Plantagenets	Hanoverians
House of Lancaster	Saxe-Coburgs
House of York	Windsors

SAXON KINGS OF ENGLAND

EGBERT: ascended throne 802. Reigned 37 years. Died 839.

ETHELWULF: ascended throne 839. Reigned 19 years. (Son of Egbert.) Died 858. Buried Winchester.

ETHELBALD: ascended throne 858. Reigned 2 years. (2nd son of Ethelwulf. Married father's widow.) Died 860. Buried Sherborne.

ETHELBERT: ascended throne 860. Reigned 6 years. (3rd son of Ethelwulf.) Died 866. Buried Sherborne.

ST ETHELRED I: ascended throne 866. Reigned 5 years. (4th son of Ethulwulf.) Died 871. Buried Wimborne.

ALFRED: born c. 848. Ascended throne 871. Reigned 30 years. (5th son of Ethulwulf.) Died 901, aged 53. Buried Winchester.

EDWARD THE ELDER: ascended throne 901. Reigned 24 years. (Son of Alfred.) Died 925. Buried Winchester.

ATHELSTAN: born 895. Ascended throne 925. Reigned 15 years. Died 940. Buried Malmesbury.

* Rule interrupted by three Danish kings.

EDMUND I: born 922? Ascended throne 940. Reigned 6 years. Died 946 (assassinated). Buried Glastonbury.

EDRED: ascended throne 946. Reigned 9 years. Died 955. Buried Winchester.

EDWY: born 940. Ascended throne 955. Reigned 4 years. Died 959, aged 19. Buried Winchester.

EDGAR: born 944. Ascended throne 959. Reigned 16 years. Died 975, aged 31. Buried Glastonbury.

EDWARD: born 963. Ascended throne 975. Reigned 4 years. Died 979, aged 16 (assassinated). Buried (i) Wareham, (ii) Shaftesbury.

ETHELRED II: born 968? Ascended throne 979. Reigned 37 years. Died 1016, aged 48? Buried St Paul's.

EDMUND: born 988? Ascended throne 1016. Reigned 1 year. Died 1017, aged 28? Buried Glastonbury.

EDWARD: born c. 1002–1007. Ascended throne 1042. Reigned 24 years. Died 1066. Buried Westminster Abbey.

HAROLD II: born 1022? Ascended throne 1066. (Brother-in-law of Edward the Confessor.) Reigned 10 months. Died 1066, aged 44? Burial place unknown, possibly Waltham Abbey.

N.B. Theory propagated by medieval chroniclers that Harold survived Hastings and lived to great age as hermit in Chester.

DANISH KINGS

CANUTE: born 995? Ascended throne 1017. Reigned 18 years. Died 1035, aged 40? Buried Winchester.

HAROLD I: born 1017. Ascended throne 1035. Reigned 5 years. Died 1040, aged 23. Buried St Clement Danes.

HARDICANUTE: born 1018. Ascended throne 1040. Reigned 2 years. Died 1042, aged 24. Buried Winchester.

Philippa, Queen of Edward III, interceding for the lives of the burghers at Calais in 1347 during the Hundred Years' War

Richard II

Henry IV

Henry V

Henry VI

Edward IV

The Black Prince
From effigy on tomb in
Canterbury Cathedral

Richard III

Unknown Flemish Artist

Henry VII
Painted 1505 when aged 48

Henry VIII

After Holbein

Artist Unknown

Edward VI

Mary I
Painted in 1544 when aged 28

THE SAXON KINGS

THE Roman occupation of England left little mark on the future. In France and Spain the effects of the Roman occupation lasted on; the very language of these countries is descended from the tongue of their conquerors. But in Britain most of what the Romans did perished after they left. Our language and our institutions are Saxon. It is therefore with the Saxons that the continuous history of England begins.

The onset of invasion by Angles, Saxons and Jutes, sea-rovers from the shores of Germany and Frisia, began about the middle of the fourth century. The Saxon conquest of England was completed within the course of the next century and a half. As bands of Saxons settled in England so 'Kings' became general. The word itself, 'Cyning', is probably connected with 'kin', indicating that the man stood at the head of his kindred or tribe. Kings were, then, in origin, mere tribal chieftains.

By about AD 600 ten separate, but not necessarily independent, kingdoms, had been established, the majority south of the Humber. The importance of seven of these kingdoms, Wessex, Sussex, Kent, Essex, East Anglia, Mercia and Northumbria, has given to the next two centuries the title of the Heptarchy.

Gradually three of the seven—Wessex, Mercia and Northumbria—began to establish some sort of domination over their smaller neighbours. Although the supremacy of individual kingdoms was usually short-lived, yet the very fact that from the late sixth century to the early ninth century they were at least nominally subject to one common overlord, was an important influence in achieving the eventual unity of England.

B

Another vital factor making for unity was the appearance of Christianity in England in AD 597. Thereafter the spread of Christianity and changes of overlordship follow almost the same course. Following the death in 616 of the King of Kent supremacy passed, along with Christianity, to Northumbria, until about 685.

Mercia, which had also put aside heathen practices, filled the position left by the decline of Northumbria, almost until the end of the eighth century. But the death in 796 of Offa, perhaps the greatest of all Saxon kings save Alfred, was followed by another southerly shift of political power, and by the end of the first quarter of the ninth century Egbert of Wessex occupied a position scarcely less secure than Offa's had been.

First King of England

It is customary to call EGBERT, 802–839, the first King of England; for although Egbert's power was not handed on intact to his successors, it was the House of Wessex which struggled valiantly to maintain the independence of England. The story of the rise and fall of Northumbria and Mercia was not paralleled in the case of Wessex, for now there was a new factor in politics. Efforts to unite England had failed hitherto, because as soon as one kingdom became great it was in the interest of the rest to pull it down. England had lacked the strongest possible motive towards union, namely the presence of a foreign foe. In Egbert's reign the Danes were already thundering at the gates; and as the dynasties of Northumbria, Mercia and East Anglia were in turn destroyed by the invader, Wessex was left to shoulder the burden alone. So it was that her leaders became the leaders of the nation.

West Saxon Kings

The outline story of the Saxon kings which follows is then the story of the 'West Saxon' kings. The period from Egbert to Edgar, covering the best part of two centuries, was the golden age of the Saxon monarchy. But the next ninety years or so, to the time of the Norman Conquest, bring the story of one calamity after another : of the inability of the later Saxon kings to preserve England from Danish ravages; of the accession of Danish monarchs to the throne; of weak kings like Ethelred and Edward the Confessor; and finally of the Norman Conquest itself.

Egbert died in 839, leaving a son ETHELWULF, who reigned till 858 (his reign is chiefly known for the bad weather periods connected with the name of his saintly adviser, Swithun). He left behind him four sons : ETHEL-BALD, 858–860; ETHELBERT, 860–866; ETHELRED I, 866–871; and ALFRED, 871–901.

ALFRED OF WESSEX, surely the most famous of all our kings, was born c. 848 at Wantage in Berkshire. He came to the throne in 871. The Danes had become settlers in Eastern England during the middle of the ninth century, had conquered most of England and were pushing southwards into Wessex. But in the year of his accession Alfred fought nine battles south of the Thames and saved his kingdom. Having stemmed the tide, Alfred busied himself with reorganising the peasant levies and laying the foundations of the English fleet. In 877 the Danes attacked his palace at Chippenham in Wiltshire and Alfred was forced to withdraw to the lake island of Athelney in Somerset—where, amongst other adventures, he is said to have 'burned the cakes'. Alfred routed the Danes in 878 at Eddington, Wiltshire, divided England with the Danish king, Guthrum, and stood godfather to the latter when he agreed to accept baptism.

But Alfred's true greatness lay in peace. He created many fortified towns, some on old Roman sites, some new ones; in all he founded some twenty-five towns, or about one-third the number founded by the Romans in three and a half centuries. He set aside a half of the revenue to be spent on educational needs; established schools where the sons of the nobility could be taught to read and write; brought in foreign scholars and craftsmen; restored monasteries and convents. He helped to design houses; invented a candle clock; mastered Latin and translated many books into Anglo-Saxon. He ordered the compilation of the first history book, the *Anglo-Saxon Chronicle*, which was continued for more than two centuries after his death. He published a collection of laws and enforced them, so that when troubles came after his death, 'men longed for the laws of King Alfred'. Had Alfred never fought a battle, he would still deserve a place among the greatest rulers of history.

Alfred the Great died in 901. The next three generations of kings were, with one exception, strong in the tradition of Alfred.

EDWARD THE ELDER, 901–925, son of Alfred, took as his title 'King of the English', not without reason; his three sons, ATHELSTAN, 925–940, EDMUND, 940–946, and EDRED, 946–955, all maintained the supremacy of Wessex against the Danes. The reign of EDWY, 955–959, reveals the tenuous nature of his supremacy. For when EDGAR, his brother, 959–975, surnamed 'Great', came to the throne, the dominions of Wessex extended only to the River Thames. Edgar, however, preserved a superficial peace.

The story of Saxon downfall begins ominously with the murder, in Corfe Castle, of EDWARD THE MARTYR, 975–979. The next ninety years to the Norman invasion of 1066 is a tale of unrelieved gloom. The grouping of events in this period reveals a certain symmetry. The long reign of the weak ETHELRED THE 'UNRAED' (ill-advised), 979–1016, is followed by a short, vigorous reign, that of EDMUND IRONSIDE, 1016–1017, and this in turn by a Danish conquest, after which the throne was occupied by Danish kings until 1042 (CANUTE, 1017–1035, and his two sons). The long reign of the weak EDWARD THE CONFESSOR, 1042–1066, is again followed by a short, vigorous reign, that of HAROLD GODWINSON, 1066, the last of the Saxon kings. And every schoolboy knows the date of the Norman Conquest.

THE NORMAN CONQUEST

It is not easy, if possible at all, to isolate and define the heritage of the Norman Conquest. For half a century before 1066 England and Normandy had been drawing closer together. Edward the Confessor himself was more Norman than English. Norman speech, habits and customs were prevalent at his court. But in the century after 1066 the followers and descendants of William the Conqueror diverted the main stream of national development and added a Latin strain to the mongrel blood of Englishmen.

Had the Conquest never happened England would probably have become part of the northern Scandinavian world. For all its cruelty the Conquest united England to Western Europe and opened the floodgates of European culture and institutions, theology, philosophy and science.

The Conquest effected a social revolution in England. The lands of the Saxon aristocracy were divided up amongst the Normans, who by c. 1087 composed between 6,000 and 10,000 of a total population of one million. More important, each landowner had, in return for his land, to take an oath of allegiance to the king, and promise to provide him with mounted, armoured knights when required. The introduction of this so-called 'feudal system', a system of land-holding in return for military obligations, provided the whole basis for medieval English society.

The Saxon machinery of government was, in large measure, retained and immensely reinforced, with a Norman monarch and the officials of his household as effective centralised controllers. Royal power was delegated in the provinces, so that government became more adequate and less capricious: rebellion from Saxon or Norman was crushed with rough but equal justice. Royal justice was not only done but was seen to be done. As well as giving the law a reputation for impartiality, the Normans brought with them their military arts—castle-building and fighting on horse-back. They revolutionised English ecclesiastical architecture—witness Durham, Winchester, Ely and St Albans, with their rounded arch-ways and doorways—introducing a standard plan for the great churches, and providing the point of depar-ture for English medieval church architecture.

The Normans also transmitted large parts of the Saxon heritage—towns and villages, shires, traditions of monarchy, the basic structure of our language. They in-herited a going, but run-down concern. They took over much that was indigenous and learnt from the con-quered. They created a strong monarchy which, in medieval times, was gradually to complete the unifica-tion of England, and obliterate the distinction between conquered Saxons and conquering Normans, so that only Englishmen remained.

The Norman Kings

WILLIAM I (THE CONQUEROR)

Born 1027. Ascended throne 1066. Reigned 21 years.

Illegitimate son of Duke Robert the Magnificent and a tanner's daughter.

Married Matilda of Flanders.

Four sons, five daughters.

Died 1087, aged 60 years. Buried St Stephen's, Caen, Normandy.

William became Duke of Normandy at the age of seven. He married the daughter of the Count of Flanders, who transferred descent in the female line from the House of Wessex.

He was second cousin of Edward the Confessor. It is said that he was promised the throne by Edward (who stubbornly refused to give his wife a child, and England an heir) in 1051. In 1064, he extorted a promise along the same lines when the unfortunate Harold Godwinson, Edward's brother-in-law, was shipwrecked in Normandy.*

On the death of Edward in 1066 the Witan chose Harold Godwinson to succeed him. William now pre-

* The descent of the throne in Saxon times bore an hereditary aspect, but there was no principle of primogeniture, e.g. in the tenth century only three out of eight kings immediately succeeded their fathers. The death of each king was followed by the election by the Witan (or council) of the most suitable candidate, royal birth being the prerequisite. After the Conquest the principle of primogeniture was gradually adopted.

pared to invade England, reciting as justification the promises of Edward and Harold.

But William was not the sole invader of England in 1066. Tostig, Harold's brother, aided by Harold Hardrada, King of Norway, landed in Northern England. Harold dashed north and defeated the invaders at Stamford Bridge, near York, on 25 September.

On 29 September William landed at Pevensey. Two weeks later, on 14 October 1066, William encountered the remnants of the Saxon army, seven miles outside Hastings, and, after a bitter fight lasting all day, in which Harold was killed, gained a decisive victory.*

The Witan now hastened to offer the throne to William as the heir of Edward the Confessor, and on Christmas Day 1066 he was crowned in Westminster Abbey.

The Conquest was not completed until about 1072, by which time regional revolts, in the North, in East Anglia —led by Hereward the Wake—and at Exeter, had been ruthlessly suppressed, bringing some semblance of order to the land.

William was now able to turn his attention to the governing of his new kingdom. The feudal tenure of land was introduced. In 1085 the Domesday survey— so called because of the searching nature of the questions—was begun, in order that taxes could be collected. All landholders were summoned to pay homage to the King at Salisbury in 1086. Lanfranc, William's new Italian Archbishop, reorganised the English Church, and

---

* Our information about William's relations with Harold, his invasion preparations and the actual Battle of Hastings, is derived from the Bayeux Tapestry. This strip of canvas, many yards long and about half a yard wide, is embroidered with detailed scenes—the first 'strip cartoon'—and is now in Bayeux Museum, Normandy.

separate Church courts were established to deal with offences under canon law, an action which was to cause much trouble for the Plantagenet Kings.

William the Conqueror, 'that stark man' as his subjects called him, was ruthless and cruel by our standards. Although only one person was executed in his reign, thousands were mutilated, especially for breaches of the game laws—the 'New' Forest was created by him as a game park: 'he loved the tall, red deer, as if he were their father'. But he was a great administrator, and gave England the first foundations of a stable and effective form of government.

He was injured at the siege of Mantes whilst fighting against his feudal overlord, the King of France. He died at the Convent of St Gervais, near Rouen, on 9 September 1087.

The *Anglo-Saxon Chronicle* gives a good impression of William's reign: 'He was mild to the good men that loved God, and beyond all measure severe to the men that gainsaid his will ... It is not to be forgotten that good peace he made in this land so that a man might go over his kingdom with his bosom full of gold ... and no man durst slay another.'

WILLIAM II ('RUFUS')

Born c. 1056–1060. Ascended throne 1087. Reigned 13 years.

Third son of the Conqueror.

Never married.

Died 1100 (accidentally shot in eye? Murdered?). Buried in Winchester Cathedral.

The Conqueror left Normandy to his eldest son, Robert, and England to his third son, William, his favourite. This arrangement was a great disappointment to Robert, a pleasure-loving knight with little control over his sparring barons. 'Rufus', so-called because of his flaming hair, was stern and avaricious, so many Norman barons took Robert's side, and risings and private wars were unceasing.

Ranulf Flambard, William's justiciar and Bishop of Durham, further angered the barons by his insistence that they pay all the feudal dues which belonged to the Crown. In order to safeguard himself against his elder brother and against a disaffected nobility, William was forced to rely on his 'brave and honourable' English subjects, especially in 1088 when he had to put down a rebellion organised by Robert.

In addition to patching up the quarrel with Robert, when the latter went off on the First Crusade (1095), William Rufus secured the frontiers with Wales and Scotland, building Carlisle Castle and a chain of forts along the Welsh border.

William's character, tyrannical, cruel and blasphemous as he undoubtedly was, has suffered at the hands of the monastic chroniclers because of the way in which he plundered the Church. Having exhausted his father's treasure, he obtained money by keeping sees vacant and diverting the revenues to his own coffers. He drove Anselm, Archbishop of Canterbury, into exile. But he was a strong, and in some ways a capable ruler, given that he neither expected nor received any co-operation from the powerful men in the country, the nobles. He was killed by a stray arrow or, as some said, was murdered, whilst hunting in the New Forest. The site of his death is marked by the 'Rufus Stone'.

HENRY I

Born 1068. Ascended throne 1100. Reigned 35 years.
Fourth son of Conqueror
Married (i) Matilda of Scotland (ii) Adela of Louvain.
One daughter, one son.
Died 1135. Buried in Reading Abbey.

Nicknamed 'Beauclerk' and later 'The Lion of Justice', the fourth and ablest son of the Conqueror succeeded his brother in 1100. Soon after his accession he married the niece of the last male descendant of the House of Wessex, for like Rufus he realised the value of English support against his own barons and against his elder brother. In 1106, Henry's army, composed largely of Saxons, defeated Robert at Tinchebrai, and until his death the unfortunate elder brother was held captive at Cardiff.

Henry further gained popularity when he recalled Anselm and issued a Charter of Liberties in which he promised to abolish the evil practices of William Rufus.

Having secured his kingdom, Henry reorganised the English judicial system and the methods of raising taxes. He created a royal court-of-all-work, the Curia Regis (King's Court), which acted as an advisory body and as a court of law and also supervised taxation. Members of this court were sent out to bring even the remote districts into contact with royal taxation, as well as to make the people familiar with royal justice. Henry's greatest agent was Roger, Bishop of Salisbury, who it is said commended himself to the King by the speed with which he could get through church services.

In 1120 Henry's legitimate son was drowned in the tragedy of the 'White Ship'. Henry nominated as his successor his daughter Matilda, who had married, as her second husband, Geoffrey, Count of Anjou—Geoffrey Plantagenet.

But when Henry died in 1135, the Council, considering a woman unfit to rule, offered the throne to Stephen of Blois, nephew of Henry and grandson of the Conqueror.

STEPHEN

Born c. 1097. Ascended throne 1135. Reigned 19 years.
Married Matilda of Boulogne.
One son, two daughters.
Died 1154. Buried in Faversham Abbey.

For seventy years after the Conquest, England enjoyed strong government and the benefits of royal justice. During the 'nineteen long winters' of Stephen's reign, England knew, once again, what it was like to be governed by a weak king.

The Welsh and the Scots invaded; and in 1139, Matilda, Henry's daughter, invaded from Anjou. The nobility, during the decade or so of civil war which followed, threw in their lot with both sides, and built castles from which they terrorised their areas. The countryside was ravaged, crops were destroyed, cattle were driven off. It was, as a chronicler put it, a time when 'Christ and his saints slept'.

In the end, the struggle for the throne was resolved by a compromise. When Stephen's son died in 1153, the two sides agreed that Stephen should retain the throne until he died (which he did in 1154), and that Matilda's son, Henry of Anjou, should then become King as Henry II.

GENEALOGY: THE PLANTAGENETS

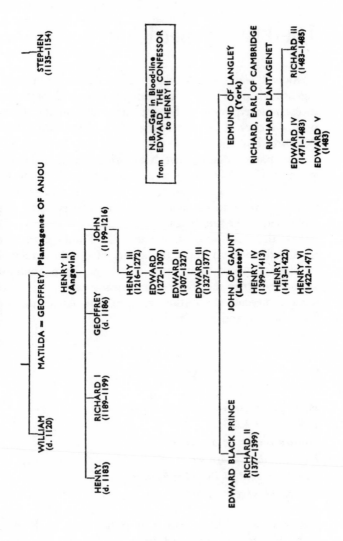

STEPHEN
(1135–1154)

WILLIAM
(d. 1120)

MATILDA = GEOFFREY, Plantagenet OF ANJOU

HENRY II
(Angevin)

HENRY
(d. 1183)

RICHARD I
(1189–1199)

GEOFFREY
(d. 1186)

JOHN
(1199–1216)

HENRY III
(1216–1272)

EDWARD I
(1272–1307)

EDWARD II
(1307–1327)

EDWARD III
(1327–1377)

EDWARD BLACK PRINCE

RICHARD II
(1377–1399)

JOHN OF GAUNT
(Lancaster)

HENRY IV
(1399–1413)

HENRY V
(1413–1422)

HENRY VI
(1422–1471)

EDMUND OF LANGLEY
(York)

RICHARD, EARL OF CAMBRIDGE

RICHARD PLANTAGENET

EDWARD IV
(1471–1483)

EDWARD V
(1483)

RICHARD III
(1483–1485)

N.B.—Gap in Blood-line
from EDWARD THE CONFESSOR
to HENRY II

The Plantagenet Kings

HENRY II was the first of a long line of fourteen Plantagenet kings. Their reigns stretched over more than three hundred years of English history, from the accession of Henry II in 1154 to the death of Richard III on Bosworth Field in 1485.

The name 'Plantagenet' was originally a nickname given to Count Geoffrey of Anjou, father of Henry II, because of the gay yellow broom flower (*planta genista*) which he wore in his helmet. In time this emblem was embodied in the family arms.

For the sake of convenience the Plantagenets are usually divided up under the names of the three related families of Anjou, Lancaster and York, from amongst whose members the fourteen monarchs came. The next section presents the outline story of the Angevins, the Lancastrians and the Yorkists.

HENRY II

Born 1133. Ascended throne 1154. Reigned 35 years.
Eldest son of Matilda.
Married Eleanor of Aquitaine.
Five sons, three daughters.
Died 1189, aged 56. Buried at Fontevrault.
First of the Angevin kings.

Henry II was a European ruler rather than an English king. His empire stretched from the Solway almost to the Mediterranean, and from the Somme to the Pyrenees. To this inheritance he added Ireland, a mission entrusted to him by Pope Adrian IV.*

The general aim of his policy in England was to undo all the harm caused by Stephen's reign. He triumphed brilliantly over the nobility, but he was, in turn, worsted by the Church.

His first concern was to restore order. Castles built by the rebellious nobles were demolished, royal castles were resumed, along with Crown lands. The northern counties were recovered from the Scots.

Henry was then able to plan for the future. He raised new taxes (scutage) from the landholders in lieu of their feudal military obligations. By a command of 1181 the basis of an English militia force was laid. Henry now had two armies: the mercenary army, paid for by the new taxes, and the militia; whilst his powerful subjects and their followers got less practice in the arts of war.

Royal justice was revived. Judges from the King's courts were again sent into the shires, where they now combined with twelve local men to administer the law; in this way Henry laid the foundations of the modern English jury system. Gradually trial by judges, with the assistance of jurymen, replaced the barbarous trials by ordeal and trials by battle, in both criminal and civil cases. (For a trial by ordeal the accused was made to plunge his hand into boiling water or carry a piece of red-hot metal. His guilt or innocence was decided by the speed with which the wounds healed.)

By the end of Henry II's reign, the English had for the first time become accustomed to paying their taxes, to co-operating in government and to expecting fair

* Pope Adrian IV, Nicholas Brakespear, was the only Englishman ever to be Pope (1154–1159).

play in the law courts. His system was so fundamentally efficient that it continued to work even under the weak rulers that followed him.

But, unjustly, it is probably for his quarrel with Thomas à Becket that Henry is chiefly remembered. The Church of England was claiming more independence from lay control than Henry was prepared to allow. He wished to retain the right to nominate to vacant bishoprics and to try in his own courts clerks* who had committed a crime, for the Church courts (introduced by William I) had no power of life and death—a cleric could only be degraded. Any wrongdoer who could read a Latin text from the Bible passed the test of clerical status (the so-called 'neck verse'), and could claim 'benefit of clergy', or immunity from the King's justice. In the same way a criminal fleeing from justice could claim 'sanctuary' in the precincts of a church.

Becket, the one-time convivial companion of Henry, turned ascetic, quarrelled bitterly with Henry over these questions, and was exiled from 1164–1170. On his return he proceeded to anger Henry still further. The murder of Becket at Canterbury Cathedral on 29 December 1170, by men believing they were acting on Henry's orders, gave the Church a martyr and ultimately a saint, whilst Henry lost all. Not until the Reformation did royal power prevail over the Church.

The closing years of the reign were troublesome. Henry's subjects on both sides of the Channel rebelled, and it was only with the aid of mercenaries and the militia that the realm was quietened at home and abroad : and the king died in 1189 knowing that his sons Richard and John had risen against him.

* A 'clerk' in the Middle Ages was anyone in orders, from the Archbishop of Canterbury to the humblest verger—about one in fifty of the population.

Artist unknown

Elizabeth I
The 'Cobham' Portrait

Artist: Daniel Mytens

James I
Painted in 1621 when aged 55

Artist: Daniel Mytens

Charles I
Painted in 1631 when aged 31

Artist: Robert Walker

Oliver Cromwell

RICHARD I (COEUR-DE-LION)

Born 1157. Ascended throne 1189. Reigned 10 years.
Second son of Henry II.
Married Berengaria of Navarre.
No issue.
Died 1199, aged 42. Buried at Fontevrault.

Richard I had little English blood in him. He was a brave soldier, but spent only ten months of his ten years' reign in England, regarding his kingdom solely as a source of revenue for his crusading ventures : 'I would have sold London itself if I could have found a rich enough buyer,' he is reputed to have said. Many towns benefited by the Charters which they gained from Richard in return for financial assistance.

Henry II had promised to undertake a crusade against the Moslems to expiate the murder of Becket, a promise not altogether disinterested, as the Angevins acquired a title by marriage to the kingdom of Jerusalem. He bequeathed this promise to his successor and, though obedience to his father's wishes had not so far been his strong point, Richard took part in the best known of all the crusades, the third.

Its aim was to free the Holy Land from the Turks, who were Moslems. It failed to do this, but Jerusalem was made easier of access for Christian pilgrims. On his way home Richard was captured by the Duke of Austria, who sold him to the Emperor Henry VI : so a crusade begun for the rescue of the Holy Land ended with the sale of one Christian monarch to another. For fourteen months, until his ransom was paid, Richard was imprisoned in a secret imperial castle, where, legend tells

C

us, he was found at last by his minstrel, Blondel. Never again did an English king leave his realm to go crusading.

Richard's absentee rule ushered in a period of some eighty years during which the Crown was weaker than in the previous century or so. The government of the country was fortunately in the hands of capable deputies, who successfully combated the ambitions of the King's brother, John, and the intrigues of the nobles, in addition to raising enormous sums of money for the expenses of the crusade and the King's ransom.

JOHN

Born 1167? Ascended throne 1199. Reigned 17 years.
Fourth son of Henry II.
Married (i) Isabel of Gloucester (ii) Isabella of Angoulême.
Two sons, three daughters by second wife.
Died 1216, aged 49? Buried at Worcester.

The archetype of the 'wicked king', John was the fourth son of Henry II, the child of his father's middle age. Not without some administrative ability, especially as regards the collection of money, he was yet cruel and avaricious.

He was nicknamed 'Lackland', because his brothers were given territory by their father when he received none. The name was soon justified, for in 1204 he lost Normandy to the King of France, and by 1205 only a fragment remained of the vast Angevin empire. In the long run this enforced insularity fostered the growth of the English nation state.

In 1205 John quarrelled with the Church, because he refused to accept Stephen Langton, the Pope's nominee, as Archbishop of Canterbury. In 1207 England was laid under an interdict, and John was excommunicated two years later. The dispute ended with John's abject surrender to Innocent III, one of the greatest of medieval popes.

The loss of England's French possessions, the ignominious failure of his quarrel with Rome, allied to misgovernment and the raising of extortionate taxes, united against John the articulate elements of society, both clerical and lay. During his absence on the Continent fighting against the French king, a project crowned with failure at the battle of Bouvines in 1214, a party led by Langton came into existence. This is the first time in English history that influential people co-operated to make a national protest against bad government.

A demand was made for the confirmation of popular liberties. On Monday 15 June 1215, on the small island of Runnymede in the Thames near Windsor, John sealed 'Magna Charta', the Great Charter, which restated the rights of the Church, the barons and all in the land.

The three most important clauses laid down

1. That the Church was free to choose its own officials.
2. That no money, over and above certain regular payments, was to be paid by the King's feudal tenants without their previous consent.
3. That no freeman* was to be punished except according to the laws of the land.

John broke his word. The nobility summoned aid from France, and John died in the midst of an invasion, bequeathing enormous problems to his nine-year-old son.

* Medieval society distinguished, of course, between servile and free men.

HENRY III

Born 1207. Ascended throne 1216. Reigned 56 years.

Married Eleanor of Provence.

Four sons, two daughters.

Died 1272, aged 65. Buried at Westminster.

Henry III was born, and spent almost his entire life, in England. He was nine years old when he came to the throne. The government of the country was in the hands of capable deputies until he came of age in 1227. During this period the French invaders were expelled and the few remaining adherents of John's party were crushed.

Then followed a period of bad government, for in spite of some redeeming features Henry was a weak, untrustworthy character. He combated his poverty, a legacy from his father and uncle, by ruthless, extortionate taxation, yet engaged in costly, fruitless wars. He filled his court and royal positions with his wife's French relations. Despite many promises of reform, nothing was done until the disaffected element in the country found a leader in the person of the King's brother-in-law, Simon de Montfort.

From 1258 England was prey to civil war; in 1264 de Montfort captured the king and Prince Edward, his son. But Henry was not deposed; he was summoned to a 'Parliament' (*parlement*, speaking), where an attempt was made to bind him to act with the advice of a council of barons. De Montfort was defeated and killed by Prince Edward at Evesham in 1265; but his Westminster Parliament, to which two knights from every shire and two burgesses from each of certain towns were summoned, marked the starting-point of the later House of Commons. His work was carried forward by Edward, his conqueror.

If he was a failure as a king, Henry III was probably the greatest of all patrons of medieval ecclesiastical architecture. During his reign the plain, massive style of the Normans gave way to the pointed arches, lancet windows, flying buttresses and elaborate decorations which are characteristic of the Early English and Gothic styles. Henry rebuilt Westminster Abbey. The majority of English cathedrals had some portion of their fabric remodelled; Salisbury Cathedral was built between 1220 and 1266.

During this long reign Franciscan and Dominican friars* set up establishments in England. This gave an impetus to works of charity and also to university teaching at Oxford and Cambridge.

EDWARD I ('LONGSHANKS')

Born 1239. Ascended throne 1272. Reigned 35 years.

Married (i) Eleanor of Castille (ii) Margaret of France.

Three sons, five daughters, by first wife; two sons, one daughter by second wife.

Died 1307, aged 68. Buried at Westminster.

Edward I was a statesman, a lawyer and a soldier. In these different capacities he cast England in the modern mould; since the Conquest, England had been in the process of crystallisation. When Edward died at the beginning of the fourteenth century, much in English government, society and law had taken on a permanent form

* 'Friar' Tuck in John's reign is an anachronism.

that in essentials was to survive the Hundred Years' War and the Wars of the Roses.

Edward was the father to the 'Mother of all Parliaments'. To his 'Model Parliament' in 1295 he summoned representatives from amongst the nobility, the greater and lesser clergy, the knights of the shires, the burgesses of the cities—thereby bringing Lords and Commons together for the first time. The growing demands on the government for justice and general administration meant that by now the feudal revenues were inadequate; Edward needed money from the new merchant class, and to summon national Parliaments was the only way to get it. Parliament became the established method of conducting public business.

Edward completed the judicial reforms begun by Henry II. The courts of King's Bench, Common Pleas and Exchequer were given separate staffs of judges and officials; and a Court of Equity, the Chancery Court, was set up to give redress where the other courts could provide no remedy.

A whole series of Acts dealt with the position of the Church, the enforcement of public order, trade and the position of great landholders. 'Conservators of the Peace' were created, forerunners of the Justices of the Peace created by Edward III.

Edward's ambition to rule over an undivided nation was checked by the independence of Wales and Scotland. Wales was conquered and brought to a tolerable state of order between 1277–1282, by the skilful use of naval and military power. The King's eldest son was created Prince of Wales in 1301, a title since borne by all male heirs to the throne.

Right until the day of his death Edward waged war unsuccessfully against the Scots, led first by Sir William Wallace and later by Robert Bruce. But the epitaph on his tomb at Westminster bears witness to the magnificence of his failure in Scotland: 'Here lies Edward the Hammer of the Scots.'

EDWARD II

Born 1284. Ascended throne 1307. Reigned 20 years (deposed).
Son of Edward I.
Married Isabella of France.
Two sons, two daughters.
Died 1327 (murdered), aged 43. Buried in Gloucester Cathedral.

Edward II was Edward I's greatest failure. Feeble and perverted, he did nothing to carry on his father's work of consolidation.

Addicted to worthless favourites, first Piers Gaveston, and later the Despensers (father and son), the King's lack of policy aroused the opposition of the nobility. Edward resorted to the noose and the block to silence his opponents. Thomas of Lancaster headed the opposition to him—the first indication of the struggle which was to develop between the Angevins and the younger Lancastrian branch of the family.

Edward was no better as a soldier than as a statesman. At Bannockburn in 1314, Robert the Bruce defeated an English army and settled the question of Scottish independence until the Union of England and Scotland in 1707.

The desertion of the Queen was followed by a swift and complete invasion by the King's opponents. Edward abdicated in favour of his son, was imprisoned, and finally was murdered at Berkeley Castle, Gloucestershire, in 1327.

GENEALOGY: THE HOUSES OF LANCASTER AND YORK

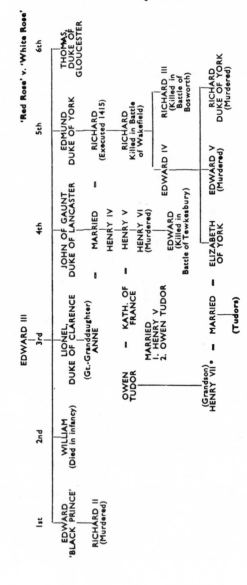

(* HENRY VII CLAIMED THE THRONE THROUGH HIS MOTHER, LADY MARGARET BEAUFORT, THE GREAT-GRANDDAUGHTER OF JOHN OF GAUNT AND HIS THIRD WIFE, KATHERINE SWYNFORD)

THE HUNDRED YEARS' WAR, 1338–1453

The struggle between England and France was carried on intermittently during the reigns of five English kings. From 1338 to 1360 the advantage lay with England. This was the period of the battles of Sluys (1340), Crecy (1346), and Poitiers (1356), culminating in the Treaty of Bretigny, 1360.

With the death of the 'Black Prince' in 1376, and the accession of Richard II (1377–1399), English fortunes reached their lowest ebb. The reign of Henry IV (1399–1413) began a period of improvement, which was continued by Henry V (1413–1422) at Agincourt (1415), and was marked by the Treaty of Troyes (1420).

The accession of the nine-months-old Henry VI (1422–1461), and the appearance of Joan of Arc in 1428, saw the tide turn in French favour. By 1453 Calais was all that remained of English possessions in France.

EDWARD III

Born 1312. Ascended throne 1327. Reigned 50 years.
Son of Edward II.
Married Philippa of Hainault.
Six sons, five daughters.
Died 1377, aged 65. Buried at Westminster.

The main interest of the long reign of Edward III lies in the opening stages of the Hundred Years' War with France. Ostensibly the war began, in 1338, to support Edward's claim to the French throne,* a pretence marked by Edward's quartering of the lilies of France beside the

* A claim not finally surrendered until 1802.

leopards of England on his coat of arms. In reality the
war was, in origin, an attempt to retain control of Gas-
cony and the wine trade centred on Bordeaux; and to
keep open the connections between the English wool
traders and the woollen markets of Flanders.

Sluys (1340), a sea battle, gave England control of
the Channel. Crecy (1346) and Poitiers (1356) demon-
strated, very convincingly, the supremacy of the English
long-bowmen over the armoured, mounted French
knights. Calais, after a twelve months' siege (1347),
passed into English hands for the next hundred years. It
was in this phase of the war that the King's eldest son,
Edward (1330–1376), known to history as the 'Black
Prince' (either because of the colour of his armour or,
more likely, because of his foul Angevin temper), covered
himself with glory.

The outbreak of bubonic plague, the 'Black Death',
in 1348–1350 removed half of the population of England and undermined military strength; in 1360 the
Treaty of Bretigny brought the war to a close. When
Edward III died in 1377 all that was left of the English
conquests were five fortified towns and the coastal lands
around them.

In England, Edward's reign saw many changes. Parliament, now divided into two Houses, met regularly to
vote supplies for the conduct of the war. 'Treason' was
defined by statute for the first time in 1352. The office
of JP was created in 1361. In 1362 English replaced
French as the official language of the law courts. Within
twenty years John Wycliffe and the Lollards (the first
'Protestants') were aiding their cause with the first
'English' translation of the Bible, and already Chaucer
was writing 'English' masterpieces. The new merchant
class and the spread of lay learning were building a
national civilisation.

RICHARD II

Born 1367. Ascended throne 1377. Reigned 22 years (deposed).
Son of the 'Black Prince', and grandson of Edward III.
Married (i) Anne of Bohemia (ii) Isabella of France.
No issue.
Died 1400 (murdered), aged 33. Buried (i) King's Langley (ii) Westminster.

Richard II succeeded his grandfather in 1377 at the age of ten, at a time of social unrest.

The Black Death had been followed by rapid increases in wages and prices. Parliament had passed legislation to restrain wages, but prices were not similarly regulated. The subsequent Peasants' Revolt of 1381, led by Wat Tyler, was put down with great severity.

Richard had only himself to blame for being 'the last of the Angevins'. He proved to be extravagant, unjust, and faithless. His only good act was to terminate the struggle with France in 1396. His final undoing was to make plain his wish to abandon Parliamentary government, now an established part of national life.

Richard's reign brought the beginning of the long struggle for the Crown between the descendants of Edward III, led first by John of Gaunt, Edward's third son and Richard's uncle, and then by Gaunt's son, Henry Bolingbroke.

On his father's death in 1399 Bolingbroke—Henry of Lancaster—returned from exile, deposed Richard and was elected King by Parliament, as Henry IV. In 1400 Richard was murdered in prison—and the Wars of the Roses had claimed their first victim.

THE WARS OF THE ROSES

The Wars of the Roses were a series of struggles for the Crown, the 'Cousins' War', which lasted over a century and affected the reigns of seven English kings, from Richard II to Henry VII.

The trouble started with Edward III's eleven children. He died leaving four surviving sons and some daughters, so that the succession could be disputed amongst too many. In addition, the marriages of royal children with the sons and daughters of powerful noble families created families which were semi-royal.

In 1399 Henry IV of Lancaster usurped the throne from the last Angevin king, Richard II. In 1461 the Yorkists in turn usurped the throne, when Edward IV deposed Henry VI. The usurpation of the Yorkist Richard III was terminated by Henry of Richmond, who was descended in the female line from an illicit union of John of Gaunt.

Henry VII's marriage to Elizabeth of York, the Yorkist heiress, united the claims of York and Lancaster, gave England the Tudor dynasty and removed the threat of further dynastic warfare.

HENRY IV

Born 1367. Ascended throne 1399 (usurper). Reigned 14 years.
Son of John of Gaunt.
Married (i) Mary Bohun (ii) Joan of Brittany.
Four sons, two daughters.
Died 1413, aged 46. Buried in Canterbury Cathedral.

'A scrambling and unquiet time'—so Shakespeare described the reign of the first Lancastrian king, Henry IV. The very nature of his accession, his usurpation of the throne when there were others with a better title, created problems for the future. From 1399 to about 1410 Henry was never free from rebellions.

Richard's half-brothers rose immediately on his behalf. The rising was put down severely, and in 1400 Richard's body was exhibited in London to disprove a rumour that he still lived.

In Wales Owen Glendower led a national rising that was not finally quelled until 1410. The Scots seized the opportunity of waging continual warfare.

The families of Percy and Mortimer, the latter with a stronger claim to the throne than Henry's, organised two rebellions. They were not quietened until 1408, and not before many nobles and the Archbishop of York had been executed for treason. There was no further outbreak of civil war until 1455.

During the last years of his reign Henry was a sick man, probably suffering from leprosy. The king who had dreamed of going on a Crusade died in the 'Jerusalem' Chamber in the house of the Abbot of Westminster in 1413.

HENRY V

Born 1387. Ascended throne 1413. Reigned 9 years.
Son of Henry IV.
Married Catherine of Valois.
One son.
Died 1422, aged 35. Buried at Westminster.

Henry V, pious, stern and a skilful soldier, succeeded his father at the age of twenty-six. The main interest of

Arms of Henry V

his reign lies outside England. He diverted England's attention away from possible internal discord by renewing the war with France; the nobles and their followers were anxious for war; Henry was equally anxious that they should not remain idle in England, and convinced himself that his cause was just. Parliament willingly voted money for Continental campaigns. The Church was appeased by the King's continued persecution of the Lollards.

Henry was more successful in the French war than Edward III at his best, and succeeded in mastering northern France. Agincourt, 1415, won in the face of tremendous odds, was only a stepping-stone to the Treaty of Troyes, 1420. By the terms of this treaty—achieved with the aid of a disaffected group within France— Charles VI, the lunatic King of France, gave his daughter Catherine in marriage to Henry, and recognised him as his heir in preference to his own son, the Dauphin. Had he lived two months longer Henry V would have been crowned King of France.

But Henry died suddenly in 1422, leaving to his baby son a claim to the French throne that would be difficult to uphold, and a nobility in England that had gained practice in the art of warfare. The son was to reap the harvest of his father's policy.

HENRY VI

Born 1421. Ascended throne 1422. Reigned 1422–1461 and 1470–1471, 40 years.

Son of Henry V.

Married Margaret of Anjou.

One son.

Died 1471 (murdered), aged 50. Buried (i) Chertsey Abbey (ii) Windsor (iii) Westminster?

Henry VI came to the throne in 1422, aged nine months. Within two months, on the death of Charles VI, he was also king of France. For the first twenty years of his reign the government of England and the conduct of the inevitable war in France were in the hands of his uncles and cousins.

With the appearance of Joan of Arc in 1428, English fortunes in France declined, and were not revived, even when the 'Maid of Orleans' was burned at the stake at Rouen in 1431. When the war at last ended in 1453, Calais was all that remained of Henry V's conquests.

In England the reign of Henry VI witnessed the most acute phase of the Wars of the Roses. The weak government was unable to control the nobles, accustomed to fighting by the long French campaign. The two aristocratic factions battled for supremacy but they left the mass of people unaffected. Peasants were gaining more freedom, and the merchant class more power.

In 1454 the King succumbed to the madness which was hereditary in his mother's family. Richard, Duke of York, next in line to the throne after Henry's son (born 1453), was appointed Regent. The King's recovery in 1455 was accompanied by the outbreak of open hostilities between the families of Lancaster and York at St

Albans in 1458. The Yorkists triumphed, Henry VI was captured and York resumed the Regency.

In 1459 a Lancastrian revival, directed by the Queen, Margaret of Anjou, who was as vigorous as her husband was weak, saw the flight of York, and his chief supporter, Richard Neville, a member of the tremendously powerful Neville family. In 1460 the Lancastrians routed the

Arms of Henry VI

Yorkists at Wakefield. York and Neville were both slain. At St Albans in the same year, a Yorkist force commanded by Neville's son was also defeated.

But this was the last real success for the Lancastrian cause. In 1461 Edward, the new Duke of York, and Neville's son, known to history as 'Warwick the Kingmaker', defeated the Lancastrians in a snowstorm at Towton. Henry VI was deposed and Edward, Duke of York, became king as Edward IV.

Between 1461 and 1470 Edward IV struggled with a new enemy, Warwick. The 'Kingmaker' was angered by the advancement of the Woodville relations of Edward's wife. He intrigued with the exiled Margaret of Anjou and the French king, Louis XI. In 1470 an invasion led by Warwick succeeded in restoring Henry VI to a puppet's throne.

Edward fled from England to Burgundy, only to return in 1471. In two battles in that year Edward regained the throne. Warwick paid the price for trying to perform the function of 'Kingmaker' to both sides, at Barnet. Henry VI's son, Prince Edward, was killed at Tewkesbury. Henry VI was probably killed after the battle by Edward IV's brother, Richard, Duke of Gloucester, of later, and greater, infamous memory.

EDWARD IV

Born 1442. Reigned 1461–1470 and 1471–1483, 21 years.

Son of Richard, Duke of York.

Married Elizabeth Woodville.

Two sons, seven daughters.

Died 1483, aged 41. Buried at Windsor.

D

Edward was far more efficient as both statesman and soldier than the tragic Henry VI had been. But his morals were poor, disapproved of even by his not very particular contemporaries, and his greed was inordinate. The English nobles also took exception to his marriage.

The undisputed rule of the first Yorkist king after 1471 can be told very briefly. Edward IV revived the old claim to the French throne and invaded France. At Picquigny in 1475 Louis XI paid 75,000 crowns and promised an annuity of 20,000, if Edward would return

Arms of Edward IV

to England. Edward was able to live on this money and the proceeds from confiscated Lancastrian estates for the rest of his reign.

One quiet event of this reign which time has proved to have been of great importance was William Caxton's return to England in 1476 after an absence of thirty-five years. He established a printing-press at Westminster from which he issued a stream of books, many of them translated from Latin and French by himself.

Edward died suddenly in 1483, leaving two sons aged twelve and nine, and five daughters.

EDWARD V

Born 1470. Ascended throne 1483. Reigned 2 months.
Elder son of Edward IV.
Died 1483 (murdered)? Buried at Westminster?

Twelve-year-old Edward V succeeded his father in April 1483. His uncle, Richard, Duke of Gloucester, the wickedest uncle of all time, had him seized from the Queen Mother's family, the Woodvilles, and sent him to the royal palace of the Tower. Edward's younger brother, Richard, Duke of York, was removed from the care of his mother, and sent to join him.

On the grounds that Edward's marriage to Elizabeth Woodville was invalid, and that his children were illegitimate, Gloucester seized the throne as Richard III.

The story of Richard's probable murder of his nephews is well known. In 1674, the skeletons of two children were discovered during the alterations in the Tower and subsequently interred in Westminster Abbey.

RICHARD III

Born 1452. Ascended throne 1483 (usurper). Reigned 2 years.
Surviving son of Richard, Duke of York, and brother of Edward IV.
Married Anne Neville.
One son.
Died 1485, aged 33. Buried at Greyfriars church, Leicester.

When he came to the throne in 1483 Richard was already credited with personal responsibility for the deaths of Henry VI, the latter's son, and his own brother

Clarence. Contemporaries, and posterity, were to saddle him with the murder of his two nephews, though his guilt is still questionable. Richard, Duke of Gloucester had proved himself an able soldier and administrator, especially in the north. His nephew's youth, and the unpopularity of the Queen Mother's Woodville relations, might have seen England fall prey once again to internal wars. So Richard III's seizure of the throne in 1483 can be defended on the doubtful grounds of 'reasons of state'.

But the murder of his nephews and the ruthless extinction of anyone who opposed his will made his rule unpopular and set afoot many plots for vengeance. Ample excuse was afforded for the invasion of Henry of Richmond, who had been in exile in Brittany. Richmond could trace his descent in the female line from John of Gaunt's illicit union with Katherine Swynford and he was 'the nearest thing to royalty the Lancastrian party possessed'.

In France he gathered a small army, Lancastrian veterans and others anxious to see the end of Richard flocking to his support. He landed at Milford Haven on 7 August 1485 and more men joined him. On 22 August at Market Bosworth, in Leicestershire, the last important battle of the Wars of the Roses was fought. Richard III was killed in battle, and Richmond became king as Henry VII.

The marriage of Henry VII to the Yorkist heiress, Elizabeth of York, united the claims of Lancaster and York and gave England the Tudor line of kings. This remarkable woman was the daughter of Edward IV, sister of Edward V, niece of Richard III, wife of Henry VII, and mother of Henry VIII; she was also a Queen of Scotland and of France.

Part Two
Tudors and Stuarts

GENEALOGY: THE TUDORS AND STUARTS

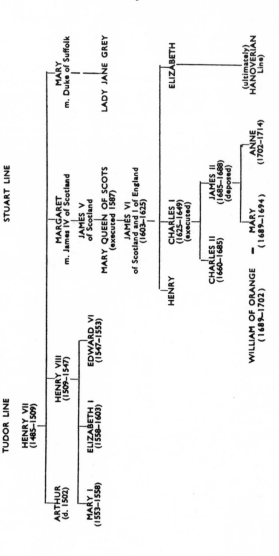

The Tudors

HENRY VII

Born 1457. Ascended throne 1485. Reigned 24 years.
Son of Edmund Tudor.
Married 1486, Elizabeth of York, eldest daughter of Edward IV.
Two sons, two daughters.
Died 1509, aged 52 years. Buried at Westminster Abbey.

As victor of the Battle of Bosworth, where Richard III was killed, Henry Tudor ascended the throne in 1485. By his marriage in 1486 with the Yorkist heiress he finally ended the Wars of the Roses. Though the Tudor dynasty began in treason and bloodshed, it brought a new, more peaceful era.

Henry was determined to restore order to the nation. By wise and firm—if sometimes avaricious—government, the old, fierce struggle between Crown and barons was ended. By heavy taxes and fines for misdemeanours, he impoverished the nobles and brought them to heel. The transitional period between the Middle Ages and Renaissance was bridged.

With the same aims, peace and prosperity, the King also steered skilfully through the complexities of European politics. His eldest son Arthur was married to the Spanish princess Catherine of Aragon, and his daughter Margaret to King James IV of Scotland.

Commerce was encouraged, and the material wealth of the country increased. In 1496 John Cabot was sent on the expedition which discovered Nova Scotia and Newfoundland; shipbuilding was encouraged with subsidies, and a start was made on establishing the Navy.

There were two insurrections during the reign. In 1487 the rebel fringe of the country put forward Lambert Simnel as the true Earl of Warwick; when their army was crushed, the boy was derisively pardoned and set to work in Henry's kitchen. Perkin Warbeck's rebellion had support from abroad; Warbeck posed as the younger of the two princes murdered in the Tower, and made repeated attempts to invade England. He was leniently treated at first, but finally imprisoned and then executed.

During the reign of Henry VII, playing cards were first invented (1486): the portrait of his wife, Elizabeth of York, has appeared eight times on every deck of playing cards for nearly 500 years.

HENRY VIII

Born 1491. Ascended throne 1509. Reigned 38 years.

Second son of Henry VII.

Married six times.

One son, one daughter, by first wife; one daughter, by second wife; one son, by third wife.

Died 1547, aged 56 years. Buried at Windsor.

The best-known fact about Henry VIII is that he had six wives. His first was Catherine of Aragon, his brother's widow, whom he married in 1509 and later divorced. The son of this union died in infancy. His subsequent marriages were to :

Anne Boleyn (mother of Elizabeth I)—beheaded.
Jane Seymour (mother of Edward VI)—died.

Anne of Cleves—divorced.
Catherine Howard—beheaded.
Catherine Parr—outlived the King.

In his early manhood Henry was accounted the most handsome and accomplished prince of his time, skilled both in learning and athletics.

Unlike his father, he was ambitious. Three years after becoming king, he invaded France, commanding the English with Austrian mercenaries, and won the 'Battle of Spurs'. In his absence the Scots invaded England and were decisively beaten at Flodden Field. James IV was killed and the flower of the Scots nobility were slain.

He wrote a book on the Sacraments in reply to Luther, for which he received the title of 'Defender of the Faith' from the Pope, a title since borne by all his successors.* His full title was: By the Grace of God, King of England, France and Ireland; Defender of the Faith and in earth under God of the Church of England and Ireland; the Supreme Head and Sovereign of the Most Noble Order of the Garter.

The failure of Cardinal Wolsey, Henry's highly influential adviser, to win the support of the Pope for Henry's intention to divorce Catherine of Aragon, led to the 'strong man's' downfall. Henry divorced the Queen, and requested Parliament to help him end financial and legal ties with a foreign power, and broke with Rome. He assumed to himself the title of Protector and Supreme Head of the Church and Clergy of England. By Royal Proclamation, a large copy of the newly translated Bible was ordered to be placed in every

* The title is still to be found on current British coinage, in the forms Fidei Defensor, Fidei Def., Fid. Def., or just F.D.

church. The Reformation in England was accomplished, though probably few people at the time realised just how drastic the upheaval had been; Henry was clever enough to represent the constitutional change as merely a reversion to the days when—he claimed—kings were masters of the English Church.

The reign saw the beginning of the great Religious Revolution : many other European states began to break away from the Roman Catholic Church and the authority of the Pope.

Henry's anti-papal campaign did not end here. The Dissolution of the Monasteries began in 1536. Henry badly needed money, and with the aid of Wolsey's successor, Thomas Cromwell, here was a harvest to be reaped. Another reason for the spoliation was that, if undisturbed, the monasteries would be hotbeds for Catholic propaganda, against Henry's break with the Papacy. The monks were indeed vulnerable to attack at this time, far too many of them being idle and immoral.

Henry carried on his father's work of creating an effective Navy. He built the *Great Harry*, of 1,000 tons, then the largest ship ever known; the first dockyard was created at Portsmouth and the Navy was separated from the Army for the first time. At his death, Henry had added some eighty ships to Naval strength and so began the challenge to the maritime supremacy of Spain. A constitutional monarch in name, he was in reality all but absolute. Nevertheless in spite of the execution of wives, ministers and clergy, he was popular with the people throughout his reign and was a brilliant statesman; at a time when Europe was in turmoil, he maintained order without an army.

EDWARD VI

Born 1537. Ascended throne 1547. Reigned 6 years.

Son of Henry VIII and his third wife, Jane Seymour.

Unmarried.

Died 1553, aged 16 years. Buried Westminster Abbey.

Edward was nine years of age when he became King, so that the country was virtually ruled by his uncle, the Duke of Somerset. This 'Protector', with Archbishop Cranmer, proceeded at once to further the religious revolution. John Knox, Ridley, Latimer and Hooper were appointed Court Preachers. Cranmer's beautifully written Book of Common Prayer (1549) was introduced to bring uniformity of worship and turned England into a Protestant state, which quickly caused a rebellion in the south-west. The gulf between Catholic and Protestant yawned wide.

Foreign policy forced an alliance between Scotland and France, and England went to war with Scotland. The general unrest led to the execution of Somerset, and

Arms of Edward VI

Northumberland—a schemer with unbridled ambition —became the strong man.

He mismanaged the country's economic situation, already bad; prices were soaring, and hardship was keenly felt among the poorer people. Disgust in agricultural areas with the enclosure of common lands, harsh rents and game laws led to Robert Kett's Norfolk rising of 1549. Soldiers went unpaid, and the Church was in chaos.

Constructive measures were few during this reign, but it is interesting to note that Sebastian Cabot (a son of John Cabot), the Bristol man, who had rendered service to Henry VII and Henry VIII, sailed with three ships and opened up trade with Muscovy, or Russia as we know it today.

Edward died of consumption in the seventh year of his reign, leaving the country torn by opposing factions.

LADY JANE GREY

Born 1537. Ascended throne 1553. Reigned 9 days. Executed 1554 aged 17 years.

At Edward's death, the next in succession was his sister, Mary. But Northumberland, anxious for his family's advancement, persuaded the dying Edward to exclude Mary from the throne on the grounds of religion—she was a staunch Catholic. Lady Jane Grey, daughter of Northumberland's tool the Duke of Suffolk, was named in her stead, and was now married to Northumberland's own son.

On Edward's death Jane was proclaimed Queen; but Northumberland was bitterly detested by many, and saw his *coup* collapse. Ten days later Mary entered London with her supporters; the people were anxious to keep a Tudor on the throne. Northumberland was imprisoned and executed. The pathetic Lady Jane and her husband met the same fate a year later.

MARY I ('Bloody' Mary)

Born 1516. Ascended throne 1553. Reigned 5 years.
Daughter of Henry VIII and his first wife, Catherine of Aragon.
Married Philip II of Spain.
No issue.
Died 1558, aged 42. Buried at Westminster Abbey (no monument).

Mary as the daughter of Catherine of Aragon had suffered an appalling childhood. Neglect, persecution and ill-health obviously had their effect in the later days of her reign.

Like her mother, she was a devout Catholic and at the break with Rome she was declared illegitimate. Though bullied and continually pressed to do so, she steadfastly refused to forsake her religion.

She was thirty-seven years of age when she entered London to meet the first challenge of her reign. Her first act as Queen was to repeal the religious legislation of her young brother's reign.

Her early marriage was considered essential and the Earl of Devon was the English candidate, but she chose instead her cousin, heir to the Spanish throne, the future Philip II who was already a widower and eleven years her junior. The Commons, realising such a match would be the greatest threat to English independence since the days of Henry III, begged the Queen to reconsider; but to bring the Catholic religion to England was undoubtedly her aim, and she stood firm. Trouble broke out almost immediately with the Wyatt Rebellion, but this was suppressed. In 1554, Philip came to England and the marriage took place at Winchester the following year.

Mary surrounded herself by zealous Catholic advisers and then attempted to enforce the wholesale conversion of England. In the succeeding years she earned her title 'Bloody' Mary. The Protestant bishops Latimer and Ridley and the sixty-seven-year-old Archbishop Cranmer were among those burnt at the stake. (The spot is marked by a bronze cross set into the roadway at Broad Street, Oxford.) The country was plunged into a bitter blood-bath, but it only served to rally more Englishmen to the Protestant faith. Calais, which had been an English possession since 1347, was lost to France in 1558.

Philip returned to Spain after only fourteenth months and Mary, after a life which had been one long tragedy, died in 1558 at Lambeth Palace.

ELIZABETH I

Born 1533. Ascended throne 1558. Reigned 44 years.
Daughter of Henry VIII and his second wife, Anne Boleyn.
Unmarried.
Died 1603, aged 70. Buried at Westminster Abbey.

Elizabeth, the last of the Tudors, found England was in a sad state. It was torn by religious fears and differences; the Treasury was empty; Calais, last foothold on the Continent, had been lost; the French King had one foot in Edinburgh. In addition, there were many who had doubts about her title to the throne.

She was a remarkable woman, noted for her learning, sometimes wayward, often wise. She loved jewels and beautiful clothes, but had a hard, sceptical intellect, coupled with a total lack of fanaticism, which helped her steer a sensible and moderate course through the conflicts of her long reign.

From first to last she was undoubtedly popular with the people and received loyalty from her statesmen. In the early part of her reign, women controlled the three important countries: Elizabeth, England; Mary Queen of Scots, Scotland; and her mother-in-law, Catherine de Medici, was Regent for Charles IX of France.

Elizabeth did her utmost to avoid war, but with the massacre of the Huguenots in France and the subsequent rise of the pro-Spanish and ultra-Catholic parties on the Continent, England felt insecure and an army went to the assistance of the French Protestants. Elizabeth aided the Spanish Netherlands (present-day Belgium) in its struggle for independence from Spain, and she refused an offer of marriage from Philip of Spain. She also skilfully assisted the Protestant cause in Scotland.

From the outset Elizabeth showed moderately Protestant inclinations, undoing Mary's church legislation and reinstating her father's.

It was an age of great adventurers and the Queen had undoubtedly a genius for the selection of capable advisers. Hawkins, Howard, Walsingham, the Cecils, Drake, Raleigh, Leicester, Essex, Burleigh, the Gilberts and many more made England both respected and feared. The disquiet caused by the massing of the Spanish Armada brought pressure on Elizabeth to allow Drake to attack Cadiz and destroy the shipping ('singeing the King of Spain's beard', he called it). Catholic plots with Mary, Queen of Scots, as their centre were repeatedly discovered and Elizabeth felt forced to execute Mary in 1587. The Armada sailed in 1588, and was decisively defeated by the skill, daring and heavier armaments of the British ships—with considerable assistance from the elements.

In this reign England's progress in the discovery and colonising field was tremendous. Raleigh's first Virginian colony was founded; Drake circumnavigated the globe, returning after a voyage of three years with $1\frac{1}{2}$ million pounds' treasure; the East India Company was founded, and English seamen left their mark in many parts of the world.

At her death, Elizabeth (who never married despite the numerous offers she received) left the country secure,

Arms of Elizabeth I

Artist: Joseph Michael Wright

Charles II

Artist: Sir Godfrey Kneller

James II
Painted in 1684 when aged 51

Studio of W. Wissing

William III

Artist: J. Closterman

Mary II

Artist unknown

Anne

Kneller
George I

Thomas Hudson—signed
George II

Studio of W. Beechey
George III

Thomas Lawrence
George IV

Franklin drafting the article of The American Independence during the war of 1775–82

Portrait: N. A. Shee

William IV

and religious troubles had largely disappeared. England was a first-class power. The Queen proved herself particularly wise in statecraft and though she held the Tudor view that the Crown had absolute supremacy over Parliament, she was tactful enough to avoid clashes between the two. The reign, too, was particularly rich in learning: it was the age of Shakespeare, Sidney, Spencer, Bacon, Marlowe and many other famous names.

E

The Stuart Kings

JAMES I (VI of Scotland)

Born 1566. Ascended throne 1603. Reigned 22 years.

Son of Mary Queen of Scots and Darnley.

Crowned King of Scotland as James VI, after his mother's abdication in 1567.

Married Anne of Denmark.

Three sons, four daughters.

Died 1625, aged 59. Buried at Westminster Abbey.

First of the Stuarts.

James was born just three months after his mother's Court favourite had been butchered to death before her eyes. His whole childhood was pitiable, spent amid a turmoil of war, murder, plot and counter-plot, among as blood-thirsty a set of intriguers as could be found.

He was crowned King of Scotland on his mother's abdication and though he made formal protests when she was executed, never showed any real feeling on the matter. He married Anne of Denmark in 1589, when he was twenty-three years of age and his bride fifteen.

A Protestant, he was nevertheless engaged continually in intrigues with Rome up to the time of the death of Elizabeth, when he became James I of England and the first King to reign over both countries. Until then English and Scots had treated each other as foreigners, and James had a hard struggle to make the English take a milder attitude to Scotland.

James had a troubled reign. He ceaselessly preached 'the divine right of Kings', maintaining that the King was above the law; the House of Commons and the lawyers firmly opposed him, denying him money to pay his debts. He had high ideals himself, but he was no statesman, and his corrupt, ill-chosen favourites and extravagant Court aroused great animosity. Macaulay said of James: 'He was made up of two men—a witty, well-read scholar who wrote, disputed and harangued, and a nervous, drivelling idiot who acted.'

In 1605 an attempt to blow up King and Parliament by Catholic sympathisers became known as the Gunpowder Plot. It failed, but brought a new wave of anti-Catholicism. The Puritans for their part were clamorous in their demands, challenging much of Elizabeth's Church settlement. Small religious groups found scant tolerance; in 1620 the Pilgrim Fathers sailed for America in their little ship *Mayflower*, seeking to found

Arms of James I. He was also James VI of Scotland, so the Unicorn of Scotland was incorporated

a community where their Calvinist tenets could flourish undisturbed. In 1611 the Authorised Version of the Bible was published, a landmark both for religion in England and for literature.

A blot on the name of James was his execution of Sir Walter Raleigh at the behest of Spain and on a charge thirteen years old.

CHARLES I

Born 1600. Ascended throne 1625. Reigned 24 years.

Son of James I and Anne of Denmark.

Married Henrietta Maria of France.

Four sons, five daughters.

Died 1649, aged 48 years (executed). Buried in Henry VIII vault, Windsor.

Charles was a weak, rickety child, but grew up to be courageous and high-minded. Unfortunately he had poor judgment, strong prejudices, and the tactlessness common to the Stuarts.

As was the practice of the day, several attempts were made when he was in his teens to arrange marriages that would form alliances, and to this end he was eventually married to Henrietta Maria, daughter of Henry IV of France. Her Catholic friends at Court much annoyed Parliament.

Early in his reign Charles encountered difficulties with Parliament, for he stubbornly refused to accept dictation. Three times it was summoned and three times dissolved, until from 1629 for eleven years he governed by personal rule. Without Parliament there was no money, but he overcame the difficulty by the sale of monopolies and the unpopular measure of 'ship' money, demanded first from seaports and later from inland towns.

Troubles with Parliament were brought to a head in 1642, when attended by soldiers Charles tried to arrest five members of the House of Commons.

Things went from bad to worse. The Civil War became inevitable, a struggle for supremacy between King and Parliament, between High Church and Puritans. In 1642 Charles' standard was raised at Nottingham, and the war began which for four long years tormented

Arms of Charles I

the realm. Very roughly the middle classes and tradesmen supported Parliament and the nobility and peasant class took the side of the King. It is estimated that the parts of country controlled by Parliament, including the ports of London, Hull, Bristol and Plymouth, contained some two-thirds of the population and three-quarters of the country's wealth; with the annihilation of the Royalist troops at the Battle of Naseby by Oliver Cromwell's New Model Army in 1645, the end was in sight.

A year later Charles surrendered himself to the Scots, who handed him over to the English. Eventually, in 1648, he was arraigned before a tribunal consisting of 135 judges, but he refused to plead. Sentence was passed, by sixty-eight votes to sixty-seven, and by one vote Charles lost his head, being executed in Whitehall.

OLIVER CROMWELL

Born 1599.

Died 1658, aged 59 years. Buried initially Westminster Abbey and after Restoration at Tyburn.

When the troubles between King and Parliament began, Cromwell was an inconspicuous Member of Parliament. His puritanical fervour and passionate oratory quickly led him to a position of eminence in the House of Commons. He had no military experience until his 44th year and at the first battle of the Civil War, was captain of a troop of horse. He later formed his invincible 'Ironsides', his New Model Army, and was a brilliant commander, a fact recognised by Parliament. In 1649, after Charles had been brought to his death, Cromwell was given command in Ireland, where Royalist campaigns were still strong; he stormed Drogheda and Wexford, massacring the garrisons with a thoroughness that has left his name for ever notorious in Irish history; he alleged that the slaughter was 'the judgment of God' upon the people. The Puritans' Act of Settlement for Ireland showed total absence of understanding of the country's needs.

Scotland, too, which was sheltering and supporting the young Prince Charles, had to be subdued, Cromwell's final victory over the Scottish rebels being as far south as Worcester.

He became Lord General of the Commonwealth and then, in 1653, Lord Protector, a position which was a virtual dictatorship, even though in theory the nation was ruled by a Council of State, comprising seven Army leaders and eight civilians. England and Wales were divided into eleven districts with a Major-General over each. Later Cromwell was offered the title of King, but the Republican section of the Army so resisted the suggestion that he declined.

Cromwell began a new foreign policy, rough but effective, designed to give England a share in the Baltic trade and to safeguard her naval supplies rather than to forward any idea of leading Protestant Europe.

At home, Parliament was proving unable to cope with the country's chaotic condition. Its outlook was narrowly Puritan—far narrower than that of Cromwell himself in some ways; for instance severe penalties were laid down for Sunday travelling or for profanity. The mass of the Army, on whose support Parliament had relied, disliked such measures; Cromwell was caught between the two, receiving much of the blame for the joyless, unsettled state of the country. A reaction set in against rule by the sword.

At his death he was buried with great pomp in Westminster Abbey, but at the Restoration his body was gibbeted at Tyburn and afterwards buried there.

His son, Richard Cromwell, succeeded to his position, but was not a strong enough character to settle such a divided nation. Army and Parliament were unable to agree on a government, and the Restoration in 1660 was more or less a transaction between Royalists and Puritans against the Army—intended more as a Restoration of Parliament than of the King himself. Richard Cromwell had to go to France, but returned, and lived peaceably through four reigns, dying in 1712 at the age of eighty-six.

CHARLES II

Born 1630. Ascended throne 1660. Reigned 25 years.
Second son of Charles I and Henrietta Maria of France.
Married Catherine of Braganza.
No legitimate issue.
Died 1685, aged 55 years. Buried at Westminster Abbey.

As a lad of twelve, Charles was with his father at the Battle of Edgehill and when the Civil War was nearing its end he escaped to France. Later, he passed to Holland and in 1650 again landed in Scotland, which country proclaimed him King of Great Britain, France and Ireland. A year later he marched into England with 10,000 men; when battle was joined with Cromwell's troops at Worcester, the Scottish Army was overwhelmingly defeated. Charles, with £1,000 on his head, was a fugitive for six weeks before he made his escape to France.

He roamed Europe for eight years, continually plotting and hoping for a Royalist rising. As the fall of the Protectorate became inevitable, Charles was invited to come back; on 29 May 1660, his thirtieth birthday, he arrived in a joyful London.

It was said of Charles that 'he never said a foolish thing and never did a wise one'. He was intelligent, tolerant and much interested in scientific developments; he submitted to working through Parliament, and concealed his yearnings for the Roman Catholic faith. When feelings ran high for retribution against the twenty-odd men still alive who had signed his father's death warrant, Charles honoured his pledge to save many of them; only nine were executed.

But he was a weak king and his foreign policy—or

rather that of his advisers—was inept. He was for ever short of money, and was at the beck and call of France, from whom he secretly accepted bribes. Dunkirk was sold to France for £400,000; after a quarrel with Holland a Dutch squadron sailed up the Thames and burned English warships at Chatham—an incident regarded as highly damaging to British prestige.

After years of war and exile, Charles had hoped for an easier life : he married the Portuguese Catherine of Braganza in 1662, glad of her dowry of £300,000 with the naval bases of Tangier and Bombay; but he also had thirteen known mistresses, including Lucy Walters (mother of James, Duke of Monmouth), Barbara Villiers (later Countess of Castlemaine) and the famous Nell Gwynne.

His niece Mary was married to William of Orange, as a diplomatic measure.

The Great Plague of London and the Great Fire took place during this reign, in 1665 and 1666. The *Habeas Corpus* Act was passed in 1679. Politics were moving into a new age, and the emergence of the two-party system, Whig and Tory, became apparent.

JAMES II (VII of Scotland)

Born 1633. Ascended throne 1685. Reigned 3 years.

Third son of Charles I and brother of Charles II.

Married (i) Anne Hyde (ii) Mary of Modena.

Four sons, four daughters, by first wife. Two sons, five daughters, by second wife.

Died 1701, aged 68 years. Buried at St Germaine (Paris).

Like his brother, James took part in the Civil War, and

when exiled took service with the French, where he distinguished himself.

James had embraced Catholicism openly when the Test Act was passed in 1673. The Act limited government offices to those who subscribed to the Anglican sacraments: James, therefore, had had to relinquish his position at the Admiralty. The violent anti-Catholic feeling which followed the Popish Plot in 1678 had made him very unpopular and he was persuaded by the King to go abroad; Charles, however, duly thwarted attempts made to exclude James from the succession.

Within six months of James's accession to the throne, another James, the Duke of Monmouth, illegitimate son of Charles II by Lucy Walters, landed at Lyme, Dorset, and was proclaimed King by Protestant adherents at Taunton. A battle fought at Sedgemoor crushed the rebellion at one stroke. Monmouth was captured, the King refused a pardon and he was executed. The uprising was followed by the 'Bloody Assizes' of Judge Jeffries and many hundreds of those who had taken part were transported for life. Some 230 were executed and many hundreds died in prison or were fined or flogged.

Religious persecution began again on a large scale. James committed every stupid error that was possible and for his intrigue with the French King, his packing of Parliament with his supporters, and the ruthless crushing of Protestantism, he became hated. He even ignored the advice of the loyal Tories.

In November 1688, William of Orange, who had married Mary, the daughter of James, landed at the head of a strong army at Brixham, Devon, to start the 'Glorious Revolution' at the invitation of Parliament, which declared that James was no longer king. At first the men of the West were slow to join William, having bitter memories of the Monmouth Rebellion, but as he neared the capital men of all parties rallied round.

James fled the country, and the throne was vacant. He made an effort to regain it later, but was heavily defeated at the battle of the Boyne in Ireland and returned to France, where he died.

WILLIAM III and MARY II

William:

Born 1650. Ascended throne 1689. Reigned 13 years.
Son of William II, Prince of Orange (of Holland).
Died 1702, aged 52 years. Buried at Westminster Abbey.
Mary:
Born 1662. Died 1694 aged 32. Buried at Westminster Abbey.
Daughter of James II and Anne Hyde.
No issue.

William of Orange was the champion of the Protestant cause in Europe. He married Mary in 1677. Despite his welcome in London, William refused to accept the vacant throne by right of conquest, he and his wife being crowned in 1689. Princess Anne, Mary's younger sister, surrendered her place in the succession to William, who would thus have the crown for life if Mary died before him; Mary did in fact die all too soon, of smallpox, in 1694.

The importance of the 'Glorious Revolution' was that the monarchy became constitutional and Parliamentary; the outstanding struggles between Crown and Parliament were over. William had been declared King by Parliament; the theory of the King as divinely ordained and set apart was finally dead.

William was a brave, unfanatical King, respected though not loved by his people. His heart lay always with the Dutch. His wife Mary was more in favour and helped win English loyalty, until her early death.

Though a Calvinist, William was impartial on religious matters; he worked hard to settle Scotland, where politics and religion were combining to produce a violent upheaval, and he established Presbyterianism there. The one blot on his name was the Massacre of Glencoe, when a Highland clan, late in making submission to him, was almost obliterated.

Jacobite plots to restore James to the throne haunted William's reign, the more dangerous being those outside the country. In 1689 James, fortified with French men and money, landed in Ireland. William himself headed an army of 36,000 men and decisively won the Battle of the Boyne; James fled to France for ever.

Arms of William III

William soon had Britain, as part of a coalition, at war with France, a war which went on ingloriously until 1697, when financial stress and diplomacy forced the allies to come to terms with their enemy.

The war of the Spanish succession brought a further menace from France, particularly with James still in exile near Paris, the centre of continual plots. Again, therefore, England went to war, this time with John Churchill, Earl of Marlborough, in command.

Marlborough had wielded considerable influence earlier in the reign. The son of an impoverished Royalist, he had helped to quell the Monmouth Rebellion in 1685, but on William's landing he had joined him, being given his title for his services. He had won the favour of the Princess Anne, who would be William's successor.

William died from a hunting accident, when his horse put a foot in a mole-hole and threw him, which incident gave rise to the Jacobite toast 'to the little gentleman in black velvet'.

William III was: William I of Ireland; William II of Scotland; William III of England; William IV of Normandy.

ANNE

Born 1665. Ascended throne 1702. Reigned 12 years.
Second daughter of James II.
Married George, Prince of Denmark.
Two sons, three daughters (twelve others died soon after birth).
Died 1714, aged 49 years. Buried at Westminster Abbey.

During the brief reign of James II, Anne had taken no part in politics; but on the landing of William of Orange she supported his accession to the throne. She was married to Prince George of Denmark—of whom Charles II had commented unkindly: 'I have tried him drunk and tried him sober, and there is nothing in him.' She had seventeen children but all died. She was thirty-seven years old when she became Queen.

Anne was closely bound to the Churchills (Marlboroughs), Lady Marlborough being a lifelong friend, and throughout her reign they exerted great influence over her and all public affairs. Political strife between Whig and Tory was keen, and was complicated by the question of who was to succeed Anne, the question which was eventually to lead to a bitter quarrel with the Duke of Marlborough.

As Commander-in-Chief, Marlborough carried on William's Continental wars of the Spanish succession with skill and vigour. His military genius dominated the scene: his popularity with the Queen, his diplomacy and his victories, kept up the country's heart for war. For ten years he won every battle he fought and secured every town to which he laid siege.

Such victories as Blenheim, Ramillies and Oudenarde brought Britain to a height of influence never before attained. Peace came in 1713, with the signing of the Treaty of Utrecht, which laid the foundation of English colonial power in the eighteenth century.

The Queen, the last Stuart sovereign, was not in any way a clever woman; but the men surrounding her were exceptional in talent. This was a brilliant age: Swift and Pope, Addison and Steele were writing in prose and verse, Sir Christopher Wren was building St Paul's Cathedral, Locke and Newton were propounding new theories.

The most important constitutional act for the reign was the sealing in 1707 of the Act of Union between England and Scotland, thus forming Great Britain.

Anne was a staunch high-church Protestant. Her creation of 'Queen Anne's Bounty' restored to the Church, for the increase of the incomes of the poorer clergy, a fund raised from tithes which Henry VIII had taken for his own use.

PRINCIPAL BATTLES, 1485–1709

Bosworth Field	1485
Flodden	1513
'Spurs'	1513
Civil War Battles	
Edgehill	1642
Worcester	1642 and 1651
Devizes	1643
Newbury	1643 and 1644
Marston Moor	1644
Naseby	1645
Sedgemoor	1685
Killiecrankie	1689
Boyne	1690
Marlborough Campaign	
Blenheim	1704
Ramillies	1706
Oudenarde	1708
Malplaquet	1709

At Sea

Cadiz	1587
Spanish Armada	1588
Beachy Head	1690

Part Three

Hanover to Windsor

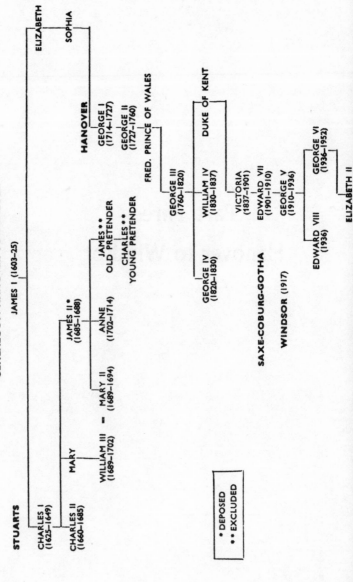

GENEALOGY: HANOVER TO WINDSOR

JAMES I (1603–25)

ELIZABETH

SOPHIA

HANOVER

GEORGE I (1714–1727)

GEORGE II (1727–1760)

FRED. PRINCE OF WALES

GEORGE III (1760–1820)

DUKE OF KENT

WILLIAM IV (1830–1837)

VICTORIA (1837–1901)

EDWARD VII (1901–1910)

GEORGE V (1910–1936)

GEORGE VI (1936–1952)

EDWARD VIII (1936)

ELIZABETH II

GEORGE IV (1820–1830)

SAXE-COBURG-GOTHA

WINDSOR (1917)

STUARTS

CHARLES I (1625–1649)

CHARLES II (1660–1685)

MARY

JAMES II * (1685–1688)

ANNE (1702–1714)

MARY II (1689–1694)

WILLIAM III (1689–1702)

JAMES ** OLD PRETENDER

CHARLES ** YOUNG PRETENDER

* DEPOSED
** EXCLUDED

Hanover to Windsor

DURING the latter part of the seventeenth century, the question which dominated all others was that of the Royal succession. In 1689, the deposed James II (1685–1688) and his infant son James (b. 1688), were effectively excluded from the throne by Act of Parliament. The Act said that henceforth no Catholic, nor anyone married to a Catholic, could be sovereign of England.

William III (1689–1702) and his wife Mary II (died 1694) had no children. When the last of Queen Anne's seventeen children, the Duke of Gloucester, died in 1701, provision for the succession had to be made. The Act of Succession, 1701, vested it in the nearest Protestant relatives of the Stuarts—Sophia, the wife of the Elector of Hanover, and her descendants. Sophia was the fifth, and only Protestant, daughter of Elizabeth of Bohemia—James I's only daughter (see the family tree). This Act deliberately passed over the superior hereditary rights of the Stuarts, represented by the Catholic James II and his son; the Hanoverian claim was purely statutory—on the score of heredity the family had no real right to the throne. (In 1910 it was estimated that there were over 1,000 descendants of Charles I who had hereditary precedence over Queen Victoria, her son and grandson.)

Sophia of Hanover died a few months before Queen Anne (1702–1714), and on 1 August 1714 Sophia's son George became the first Hanoverian King of England as George I. Hanover was an offshoot of the duchy of Brunswick-Luneberg, which had been governed by the Guelph family since the twelfth century; hence the

Hanoverian kings were referred to in England as Hanoverians, as Guelphs or as the House of Brunswick.

The joint rulers of England and Hanover were:

George I	(1714–1727)
George II	(1727–1760)
George III	(1760–1820)
George IV	(1820–1830)
William IV	(1830–1837)

The accession of Queen Victoria in 1837 saw the separation of England from Hanover, which had become a kingdom in 1814. As the succession to the throne of Hanover was governed by the Salic law and therefore could not pass to a woman, it passed to the nearest male relative, Ernest, Duke of Cumberland, fifth son of George III; and to mark the change the German arms were removed from the Royal arms of England, leaving them as they are today. Hanover was later swallowed up in Bismark's Germany.

Edward VII, the eldest child of Queen Victoria and the Prince Consort, took his father's family name—that of Saxe-Coburg-Gotha—but popularly the Royal family was still known as the House of Hanover or Brunswick. In July 1917, during World War I, King George V announced that he had abandoned all German titles for himself and his family, who would be known henceforth as the House of Windsor.

GEORGE I

Born 28 March 1660. Ascended throne 1714. Reigned 13 years.
Son of Ernest, Elector of Hanover.
Married Sophia, Princess of Zelle (1682).
One son, one daughter.
Died 11 June 1727, aged 67. Buried in Hanover.

Under the terms of the Act of Settlement, 1701, George Louis of Brunswick-Luneburg, who had become Elector of Hanover in 1698, became King of England when Queen Anne died.

George I saw clearly that the Hanoverians had been brought in by the Whigs,* in preference to the Catholic Stuarts, merely as the lesser of two evils. Any line of action he initiated was likely to offend at least half the country. In fact 'George, aged fifty-four when he became King, never even took the trouble to learn the English language and spent more time in Hanover than in England. His character was in any case ill-suited to the position.

The Court, always the centre of government, virtually ceased to exist. George brought to England two mistresses but no wife: he had married his cousin Sophia in 1682, and dissolved the marriage in 1694. Sophia, on suspicion of adultery, was kept in strict confinement until her death in 1726. The two children of the marriage were the future George II and Sophia Dorothea, who was to be the mother of Frederick the Great of Prussia. Between George I and his son began that hostility between sovereign and heir-apparent which was to become traditional in the House of Hanover.

George was only too content to leave the conduct of affairs in the hands of ministers, thereby transferring to their shoulders the responsibility for national policy. In choosing his ministers from among the Whigs, George laid the foundations of the Whig oligarchy which ruled England for the next fifty years. Cabinet government began in this reign, and Sir Robert Walpole (1676–1745), the chief minister of the majority party in the

* The terms Whig and Tory were both originally terms of contempt, coined in the late seventeenth century. Whigs were Scottish 'whiggamores' or horse-drovers; Tories 'Irish robbers.'

Arms of George I (Hanover)

House of Commons, became England's first Prime Minister. His great chance came when the 'South Sea Bubble' burst in 1720: the South Sea Company, a highly speculative venture, had persuaded even the Government to become involved with its schemes; Walpole had strongly advised against it, and as First Lord of the Treasury he was able to salvage something from the wreckage.

In 1715 the Jacobites, still supporting the Catholic Stuart line, attempted to supplant George I by James Edward Stuart, the 'Old Pretender', the son of James II. The rebellion failed miserably: the Pretender did not arrive in Britain until it was over, and help promised by France never materialised because of the death of the French King, Louis XIV. As a political force, Jacobitism was now dead.

George I died at Osnabrück on 11 June 1727 while on his way to his beloved Hanover.

GEORGE II

Born 10 November 1683. Ascended throne 1727. Reigned 33 years.

Only son of George I.

Married Caroline of Anspach (1705).

Three sons, five daughters.

Died 25 October 1760, aged 76. The last English king to be buried at Westminster.

George II, like his father before him, was first and foremost a German prince; but at least he knew England before he was too old to learn. He, too, had to rely on the Whigs, led at first by Sir Robert Walpole—to whom the Queen, Caroline of Anspach, was a loyal and clever adviser. Unlike most Hanoverian kings, George was devoted to his wife, who unfortunately died in 1737. There was, however, the usual Hanoverian friction between father and son, ended abruptly in 1751 with the death of Frederick, Prince of Wales. A contemporary wrote the epitaph :

Here lies poor Fred who was alive and is dead,
Had it been his father I had much rather,
Had it been his sister nobody would have missed her,
Had it been his brother, still better than another,
Had it been the whole generation, so much the better
for the nation,
But since it is Fred who was alive and is dead,
There is no more to be said.

Walpole's methods were crude but efficient; he gave England a welcome period of peace, and firmly established the system of government through a Cabinet responsible to a Parliament, which was in turn responsible to the electorate. Also, as during the reigns of both

George I and George II the Tories were suspect because of their associations with Jacobitism, the custom was established that the Cabinet should consist of men of only one political party.

Against Walpole's wish, war on Spain was declared in 1739, the beginning of a series of wars which was to last intermittently until 1815. In 1742 Walpole had to resign, dying three years later. The war extended, becoming the war of the Austrian succession, aimed largely against France; and at the battle of Dettingen, in 1743, George II achieved the distinction of being the last reigning monarch to lead his subjects in the field.

In 1745 the Jacobites tried once again to restore the Stuarts to the throne. Prince Charles Edward Stuart, the 'Young Pretender', grandson of James II, landed in Scotland. A year later he was routed at Culloden Moor by the Royal Army under the king's second son, the Duke of Cumberland—'Butcher Cumberland'.* Bonnie Prince Charlie escaped, lurking for six months in the Western Isles under the care of such loyal followers as Flora Macdonald; no one betrayed him, though a price of £30,000 was on his head. He moved later to France, finally dying a drunkard's death in Rome.

In 1756 the Seven Years' War with France began, initially because of clashes in North America, though rivalries were also fierce in India, and fighting swept into Europe too. The British suffered severe reverses, and the government broke up; against the King's wishes, William Pitt the Elder (1708–1778), later Earl of Chatham, emerged as leader to meet the crisis.

George II died at Kensington on 25 October 1760, before the Seven Years' War reached its successful conclusion in 1763.

* The flower 'Sweet William' was named after him; in Scotland it is called 'Stinking Billie'.

The Change of Calendar, 1752

Julius Caesar in 46 BC fixed the length of the year at 365 days, and 366 days every fourth year. The months had thirty and thirty-one days alternately, with the exception of February (then the last month of the year), which had twenty-nine in ordinary years, and thirty in Leap years. To mark this change of calendar July was named after its originator.

The Emperor Augustus upset this arrangement by naming August after himself, and in order that it should have the same number of days as July, i.e. thirty-one, took one day from February in both ordinary and Leap years.

The *Julian* Calendar made a slight error in the length of the year, a mere eleven minutes and fourteen seconds; but by the sixteenth century the cumulative error was about ten days. This was rectified by Pope Gregory XIII who, in 1582, decreed that 5 October should become the fifteenth. In order to prevent a recurrence of the fault it was ordained that the centurial years (i.e. 1600, 1700, etc.) should not be Leap years unless divisible by 400.

England did not accept this *Gregorian* calendar until 1752, thereby causing much confusion between English and Continental dates, whilst the disparity between the Julian and Gregorian calendars was now eleven days. An Act of Parliament in 1750 made 2 September 1752 into 14 September and moved the first day of the year from 25 March (still reckoned as the beginning of the financial year) to 1 January.* In this way England was brought into line with the rest of Europe.

* 24 March 1700, for example, was followed by 25 March 1701.

GEORGE III

Born June 1738. Ascended throne 1760. Reigned 59 years.
Grandson of George II.
Married Charlotte of Mecklenburg-Strelitz (1761).
Nine sons, six daughters.
Died 29 January 1820, aged 81. Buried at Windsor.

The twenty-two-year-old King determined to rule as well as to reign. He wished to recover the power of the Crown from the Prime Minister, and he temporarily succeeded in doing so. Parliament had no great popular support in the country, as too many MPs sat merely at the bidding of an individual patron. William Pitt, elected Prime Minister to meet a war crisis, which he did brilliantly, was unpopular afterwards with the Whigs in power. During the first two decades of his reign, George worked methodically to break the power of the Whigs which had lasted since 1714. He used bribery to create his own party, the 'King's friends', and directed the country through the medium of carefully selected Whig ministries, which he changed frequently, until he was strong enough to appoint his own minister, Lord North.

George III and Lord North must bear the responsibility for the loss of England's North American colonies. The colonists were exasperated by repeated attempts by the British government to impose taxes on them. Their anger found outlets in incidents like the 'Boston Tea Party' (1773), and in 1775 war broke out. The colonists proclaimed their independence on 4 July 1776, and achieved it at the Peace of Versailles signed in 1783. George's obstinacy in dealing with people whom he believed to be rebels had much to do with the causes of the war and its needless protraction. The Whigs in general had no clear ideas on colonial policy; they still thought of colonies merely as markets for British goods. But they soon saw that the recovery of the American colonies was impossible and refused to support the King in continuing the war.

This brought to an end George III's period of personal rule. In 1783 he resigned much ministerial power to the twenty-four-year-old William Pitt the Younger (1759–1806), famous son of a famous father; a Tory, he was to be Prime Minister with only one break (1801–1804) until his death in 1806.

George III had married Charlotte of Mecklenburg-Strelitz. He was devoted to her and at first to their fifteen children (nine sons and six daughters), but the tradition of hostility between the reigning monarch and the heir-apparent later developed strongly.

The King was highly neurotic with a flair for music, furniture and gardens; he liked making buttons and putting watches together. He was keenly interested in the agricultural improvements which took place during his reign; and the creation of model farms on his estate at Windsor earned him the nickname of 'Farmer George'. He was a patron of the sciences and the arts, and his collection of books laid the foundation for the future British Museum Library.

During the closing years of his reign, he had little influence on English affairs. His mind had always been weak and vindictive, and after 1811 he was at times both blind and insane. His eldest son George ruled for him as Prince Regent.

England was guided through the long French Revolutionary and Napoleonic Wars (1793–1815) by Pitt and the military and naval genius of such men as the Duke of Wellington (1769–1852) and Lord Nelson (1758–1805). In 1801 the Act of Union joined Ireland to

England until the Government of Ireland Act, 1920, established the modern arrangements. In 1807 the slave trade was abolished in lands under British control, but slavery continued in British possessions until 1833.

Besides great statesmen like Pitt and Fox, and great captains like Wellington and Nelson, George III's long reign was graced by some of the greatest names in English literature : Johnson, Gibbon, Cowper, Crabbe, Scott, Jane Austen, Byron, Coleridge, Wordsworth, Southey, Shelley and Keats. Artists like Reynolds (the first President of the Royal Academy, founded 1768), Gainsborough and Romney founded a school of English painters.

There were many changes in England during the eighteenth century. The population more than doubled, stimulating far-reaching changes in agriculture and industry in order to keep pace with the growing demands for food and manufactured goods. Transport was revolutionised, with new roads and the first canals.

George III died on 29 January 1820, having spent the last nine years of his reign in seclusion. He was succeeded by his eldest son George, the Prince Regent, as George IV.

French Revolutionary and Napoleonic Wars 1793–1815

In 1793 England and a coalition of other European powers went to war against the French revolutionaries who, having seized power in France, seemed bent on conquering Europe. By 1797 England was alone against the all-conquering French Republic. 'England's Blackest Year', 1797, proved to be the turning-point of the war. Naval victories at Camperdown and Cape St Vincent*

* William, Duke of Clarence, later William IV, fought in this battle.

gave England naval supremacy, which was consolidated in 1798 at the battle of the Nile, and at Copenhagen in 1801. England was now supreme at sea, and the French on land. Peace was made at Amiens in 1802.

Napoleon Bonaparte (1769–1821) who had seized supreme power in France in 1801 and who was to become Emperor in 1804, used the next few months to reorganise French fighting forces prior to launching an attack against England. War was renewed in 1803. For two years Napoleon tried to invade England, but his schemes were ruined by Nelson's defeat of the combined French and Spanish fleets off Cape Trafalgar in 1805.

Napoleon then resorted to economic warfare in an attempt to bankrupt the 'nation of shopkeepers', but England's Navy frustrated his plans; and the subject-nations of Europe grew restless under the French yoke. First Spain and Portugal and then Russia revolted, and Napoleon was forced into the Peninsular War, 1808–1814, and the disastrous Moscow campaign of 1812. The English blockade of Europe at this time caused much trouble with neutral countries, and the Anglo-American War, which broke out in 1812, lasted until 1814.

Peace negotiations with the French were opened in 1814. Napoleon was exiled to Elba from where he escaped, returned to France, and began his 'Hundred Days Campaign' which ended at Waterloo, 1815. He was exiled to St Helena, where he died in 1821.

GEORGE IV

Born 12 August 1762. Ascended throne 1820. Reigned 9 years. Eldest son of George III.

Married (i) Mrs Maria Fitzherbert (1785) (ii) Caroline of Brunswick-Wolfenbuttell (1795).

One daughter.

Died 26 June 1830, aged 67. Buried at Windsor.

'He will be either the most polished gentleman, or the most accomplished blackguard in Europe—possibly both,' said the tutor of the future George IV when he was fifteen.

From Carlton House, where he set up his own establishment in 1783, 'the first gentleman of Europe' became the leader of gay London society, setting the fashion in dress and patronising the arts and architecture. He 'discovered' Brighton and had the Pavilion built in 1784. Regent Street and Regent's Park were laid out and named after him; the term 'Regency style' passed into our language.

Both before and during his reign, George IV did much harm to the cause of monarchy. Subjects who had grown accustomed to the irreproachable family affairs of George III were exasperated by his immorality. His reckless extravagance was the more conspicuous at a time when the after-effects of the Napoleonic Wars and the upheavals of industrial revolution were causing much social distress and misery. He was a great embarrassment to Lord Liverpool's government, which though committed to *laissez-faire* economics and far from reform-minded, was concerned to reduce costs and ease poverty.

George had a steady flow of mistresses while he was Prince Regent; this was stemmed in 1785, when he married secretly a twice-married young Catholic widow, Mrs Maria Fitzherbert. Since he married without his father's permission, the union was illegal; in any case a prince married to a Catholic would not be allowed to succeed to the throne.

So in 1795, in order to placate his father who refused to settle his debts on any other terms, George married his cousin, Caroline of Brunswick. He treated her abominably throughout their married life together, which barely survived the birth of their only child early in 1796. His attempts to divorce his wife disgusted the country.

From 1811, as the Prince Regent, he was King in all but name. The death of George III in 1820 gave him the title of King without altering in any way the situation which had existed since 1811. George IV's first care at his accession was to attempt to exclude his wife's name from the traditional prayers offered for the Royal family; and he did succeed in having her excluded from his Coronation in July 1821.

But George IV was very intelligent and had great aptitudes; his faults were the result of much indolence and lack of application. He had great literary taste and appreciation; he was a fervent admirer of Jane Austen and kept a set of her novels in each of his residences. 'I shall always reflect with pleasure,' he said, 'on Sir Walter Scott's having been the first creation of my reign.' He gave George III's library to form the basis of the British Museum Library; and persuaded the government to buy the Angerstein collection of pictures which pioneered the National Gallery. George was, in addition, probably the wittiest of all English monarchs, Charles II excepted.

'He was the most extraordinary compound of talent, wit, buffoonery, obstinacy and good feelings, in short, a medley of the most opposite qualities, with a great preponderance of good—that I ever saw in any character in my life,' was the comment of the Duke of Wellington.

George IV died on 26 June 1830, an event hailed with relief. He was succeeded by his brother, the Duke of Clarence, as William IV, because his only legitimate child, Princess Charlotte, had died in 1817.

WILLIAM IV

Born 21 August 1765. Ascended throne 1830. Reigned 6 years.
Third son of George III.
Married Adelaide of Saxe-Coburg and Meiningen (1818).
Two daughters.
Died 20 June 1837, aged 71. Buried at Windsor.

Following the death of Princess Charlotte in 1817, William, Duke of Clarence, and his brothers, the Dukes of Kent and Cambridge, were prevailed upon to quit their middle-aged semi-retirement in order to secure the succession. When his elder brother, the Duke of York,* died in 1827, William became heir to the throne.

On his accession in 1830, William IV was very popular. His unassuming character, exemplary private life (at least since his marriage; from 1790 to 1811 he had lived with the actress Mrs Jordan, by whom he had had ten children) and his known hatred of pomp and ceremonial (he even wanted to dispense with the Coronation) rendered him an agreeable contrast to George IV.

The great question in 1830 was Parliamentary reform. George IV had been resolutely opposed to any and every reform—though Roman Catholic Emancipation had been won in spite of him in 1829. William IV was more liberal in his attitude. After a difficult passage a Reform bill was piloted through the Lower Chamber in 1831, but its continual rejection by the Lords brought England to the verge of revolution. The new, articulate middle-class insisted that no longer could the hereditary land-owners remain solely responsible for a nation so urgently needing financial, economic and social overhaul. William

* The 'Noble Duke of York' of the nursery rhyme, C-in-C British Army 1798–1827. He was no military general but a very able administrator.

Portrait: A. E. Penley

Queen Victoria (four years after Accession)

The influence extended by Queen Victoria over the members of the European monarchy can be gauged from the above picture, c. 1872, of members of the Royal Family

Four generations: Queen Victoria nurses her great-grandson, Albert Edward, later Edward VIII; standing, Edward (later Edward VII) on the left and George (later George V)

Queen Victoria opening the Great Exhibition of 1851 when Britain was at the height of her power. The Exhibition was the inspiration of Albert, Prince Consort, seen on the right of the dais

IV, refusing to be hurried into the wholesale creation of Whig peers to swamp the Tory majority in the Lords, used his personal influence to obtain majority support for the measure in the Lords; the Reform Act was passed in 1832. This extended the franchise to the middle-classes on the basis of property qualifications; it left the working-classes bitterly disappointed,* but it did mean that the landowning class had at last decided to share government with the more prosperous tenant farmers, skilled artisans and industrialists.

In 1833 slavery was abolished in British colonies, thereby completing the work begun in 1807; the government set aside twenty million pounds as compensation for the slave owners. The Poor Law was reformed in 1834, for the first time since 1601—although this measure created the workhouse system, so graphically depicted by Dickens in the pages of *Oliver Twist*. Local government was reformed in 1835.

It was probably because William IV was one of the least remarkable of all English sovereigns that England passed unscathed through a period of revolution which threw other European countries into turmoil. He was the only European monarch of that date to survive the advent of democracy.

William IV died on 20 June 1837, and was succeeded by his niece, the Princess Victoria of Kent.

VICTORIA

Born 24 May 1819. Ascended throne 1837. Reigned 63 years.
Granddaughter of George III.

* Subsequent Acts of 1867, 1884, 1918 and 1928 gradually extended the franchise, until by 1928 all men and women over the age of twenty-one had a vote.

G

Married Prince Albert of Saxe-Coburg-Gotha (1840).
Four sons, five daughters.
Died 22 January 1901, aged 81. Buried Frogmore, Windsor.*

> I sing the Georges four,
> For Providence could stand no more.
> Some say that far the worst
> Of all was George the First.
> But yet by some 'tis reckoned
> That worse still was George the Second.
> And what mortal ever heard,
> Any good of George the Third?
> When George the Fourth from earth descended,
> Thank God the line of Georges ended.
> (Walter Savage Landor, 1775–1864)

Landor's bitter lines give some indication of eighteen-year-old Queen Victoria's heritage in 1837. William IV had been a great improvement on his brother, but he was not an impressive figure. The throne which Queen Victoria inherited was weak and unpopular and it took her a long time to live down the irreverence with which the nation had treated her Hanoverian uncles. Early in her reign the London mob shouted 'Mrs Melbourne' after her at the time of the 'Bedchamber Crisis'. This was because the Queen had refused to change her ladies-in-waiting after the fall of Melbourne's government.

Queen Victoria was the only child of the second marriage of Princess Victoria of Saxe-Coburg to Edward, Duke of Kent, fourth son of George III. Her father died when she was eight months old, and his place was filled by her uncle Leopold of Saxe-Coburg (later king of the Belgians). He was responsible for the general character of her early education.

In February 1840 the Saxe-Coburg influence upon

* The Queen did not wish to be buried amongst her Hanoverian uncles.

her life was strengthened by her marriage to her cousin, Albert of Saxe-Coburg-Gotha (1819–1861). Tactless, serious, conscientious and very German, Albert never endeared himself to the English people. There was no precedent, maintained the Archbishop of Canterbury, for his being included in the customary prayers for the Royal family; he was excluded from any official position in the political life of the country; although he was made a British citizen, he was never granted the titular dignity of an English peer; nor, until he and Queen Victoria had been married for seventeen years (1857), was he made Prince Consort. Prince Albert, however, did quietly exert tremendous influence over the Queen, and until his death he was the virtual ruler of the country.

He proved to be a devoted husband and father, and helped to raise the monarchy to the lofty pinnacle of respectability where it has since remained. He left two permanent legacies to England : one was the Christmas tree, which he introduced from his native Germany; the other grew out of the Crystal Palace Exhibition of 1851. Six million people visited the Exhibition, which showed a profit of £186,000. With the money, thirty acres of land were purchased in Kensington, to be de-developed as a shrine to science and art. This land now bears, amongst similar institutions, the Victoria and Albert Museum, the Science Museum, the Imperial College of Science and Technology, the Royal College of Music and the Royal Albert Hall.

The death of the Prince Consort on 14 December 1861 was followed by the Queen's withdrawal to the seclusion of Osborne, Balmoral, Windsor or the Riviera, for a period of mourning which, despite public criticism, lasted until the Golden Jubilee celebrations in 1887.

During her seclusion the Queen was not inactive. Her husband had taught her to be a conscientious public servant, and she gave close attention to daily routine business and administration, at a time when great political and social reforms were transforming England. The chief advances through legislation were the Mines Act (1842) forbidding the employment of women and children underground; various factory acts which eventually established a ten-hour day; the Education Act of 1870; the Public Health and Artisans' Dwelling Acts (1875); Trade Union Acts (1871 and 1876) and the Reform Acts of 1867 and 1884 which widened the franchise.

These acts were implemented by the ten Prime Ministers of her reign : Lord Melbourne, Sir Robert Peel, Lord John Russell, Lord Derby, Lord Aberdeen, Viscount Palmerston, Benjamin Disraeli, William Ewart Gladstone, Lord Rosebery and Lord Salisbury. Melbourne and Disraeli probably had the greatest influence over the Queen. She disliked Gladstone intensely; she once complained that he addressed her as if she were a public meeting.

During her reign the British Empire doubled in size. New Zealand became a part in 1840, Canada a Dominion in 1867 and Australia a Commonwealth in 1900. The Empire was consolidated and expanded, though with much more difficulty, in Burma, the Pacific, Egypt, South Africa and India. Wars were fought in Egypt and South Africa (Boer Wars in 1881, and 1899–1902), and a mutiny suppressed in India (1857), before English rule was finally established in those countries. In 1875 Disraeli obtained the controlling interest in the Suez Canal. In 1876, the Queen became Empress of India. Apart from participation in the Crimean War (1853–1856), during which the Queen introduced the Victoria Cross, England was involved in no major European entanglements between 1815 and 1914.

The Queen's unique position at the head of one large European family of royalty was probably a contributory factor in keeping her country at peace. She was related, either directly or by marriage, to the royal houses of Germany, Russia, Greece, Rumania, Sweden, Denmark, Norway and Belgium. The Tsar of All the Russias was her 'dear Nicky', and the Emperor of Germany, the dreaded Kaiser Wilhelm II, was 'Willy', her own grandson. Queen Victoria ruled her own, and this wider European family, despotically.

The Queen's tastes, her virtues and her limitations, reflected those of the middle-class generally. She disliked all 'modern' music ('You couldn't drink a cup of tea to that,' she remarked of a drinking-song by Rubinstein); she found 'modern' paintings odd. But she was the first sovereign to travel in a railway train, and the first British sovereign to visit France officially (1855) since the coronation of Henry VI in 1431.

Queen Victoria died in the sixty-fourth year of her reign* on 22 January 1901 : it was not just the end of a reign, it was the end of an era. She had reigned three years longer, and was three days older at the time of her death, than George III. During that time France had known two dynasties and become a republic; Spain had seen three monarchs and Italy four. She was succeeded by her eldest son as Edward VII.

Queen Victoria was survived by six children, forty grandchildren and thirty-seven great-grandchildren—including four future sovereigns of England, Edward VII, George V, Edward VIII and George VI.

---

* Longest reigns: Louis XIV of France, born 1638, reigned for seventy-two years, 1643–1715.

Francis Joseph, Austrian Emperor, born 1830, died in 1916 after a reign of sixty-eight years, 1848–1916.

The Family of Queen Victoria and the Prince Consort

1. Princess Victoria (1840–1901) married Emperor of Germany, mother of Kaiser Wilhelm II. A daughter married King of Greece.
2. Edward VII (1841–1910) married daughter of King of Denmark. A daughter married King of Norway.
3. Princess Alice (1843–1878) married Duke of Hesse-Darmstadt. A daughter married the ill-fated Tsar Nicholas II of Russia, and was assassinated with him and other members of the Russian Royal family in 1918. A granddaughter of Princess Alice married a future King of Sweden; Lord Louis Mountbatten is her grandson and H.R.H. Prince Philip, Duke of Edinburgh, her great-grandson.
4. Prince Alfred (1844–1900) married daughter of Tsar Alexander II. A daughter married King of Roumania. A granddaughter married King of Yugoslavia.
5. Princess Helena (1846–1923) married Prince Christion of Schleswig-Holstein (German principality).
6. Princess Louise (1848–1939) married Duke of Argyll.
7. Prince Arthur (1850–1942) married Princess Louise of Prussia.
8. Prince Leopold (1853–1884) married Princess Helena of Waldeck (German principality).
9. Princess Beatrice (1857–1944) married Prince Henry of Battenburg. A daughter married Alfonso XIII, the last King of Spain.

EDWARD VII

Born 9 November 1841. Ascended throne 1901. Reigned 9 years. Eldest son of Queen Victoria.

Married Alexandra of Denmark (1863).
Three sons, three daughters.
Died 6 May 1910, aged 68. Buried at Windsor.

Edward was the first heir born to a reigning monarch since 1762. He was educated privately, and at the universities of Edinburgh, Oxford and Cambridge. Even after the death of his father in 1861 he was consistently denied any share in government, for his mother continued in the attitude of suspicion towards the heir-apparent which had marked all the rulers of Hanover. The Prince of Wales, denied outlet for his energies, dissipated his great and growing powers in petty and unsuitable pursuits; this is the possible explanation of the Tranby Croft scandal and of his appearance in the Mordaunt divorce case.

At the age of fifty-nine Edward VII, a grandfather, came to the throne. It was soon apparent that Queen Victoria's usually sound judgment had been seriously at fault for, as King, Edward VII soon displayed the greatest skill in dealing with his ministers and with foreign rulers.

The field of foreign affairs was his *forte*. His world-wide travels, made as Prince of Wales to Italy, Spain, America, Canada, India, Egypt and the Holy Land, Ireland, Denmark, France, Germany, Belgium and Russia, forged many useful links abroad. Within two years of his accession he had become known as 'Edward the Peacemaker', a well-deserved tribute to his constant attempts to foster international friendliness. In 1902 the Boer War ended, but the European situation was ominous and England isolated. The 'Entente Cordiale' with France in 1904 owed much to the King's initiative and diplomacy.

The reign of Edward VII saw important changes in

England. During the last two decades of Queen Victoria's reign there had been a dearth of social legislation (successive Liberal and Conservative Governments had been wrestling with the problem of Ireland, and Lord Salisbury did not believe in social improvement by legislation) and there was much lee-way to be made up. In 1902, an Education Act provided secondary education at the State's expense. The Liberal Government after 1906 passed a series of reforms to benefit children, introduced old-age pensions (1908) and Labour Exchanges (1909), and laid the basis for the National Insurance scheme which was to be enacted early in the next reign. The money for these schemes was budgeted for in 1909; and the Lords' rejection of the Budget in that year sparked off a constitutional crisis.

A Saxe-Coburg by birth, upbringing and in appearance, Edward VII was really a Hanoverian. He possessed the social graces, shrewdness and care for personal appearance which had characterised that family; he set the fashions of the day. But he also had tact, warmth and consideration for others, qualities in which the Hanoverians had been markedly deficient. His affability and dandyism made him a popular figure with the majority of his subjects; although his indiscretions probably caused him to forfeit the support of the middle classes.

Edward VII's sporting interests and activities had much to do with his popularity. His racing yacht *Britannia* was one of the most successful of her day, and the King was very successful on the turf. He became the first reigning monarch to win the Derby, with *Minoru* in 1909.

Edward VII married Alexandra, daughter of Christian IX of Denmark, in 1863. There were six children of the marriage : his eldest son, the Duke of Clarence, who died in 1892; the Duke of York, who succeeded his father as George V in 1910; the Princess Royal, who married the Duke of Fife; Princess Victoria; and Princess Maud, who married King Haakon VII of Norway.

King Edward died in the middle of a constitutional crisis, on 6 May 1910. Nine crowned heads of Europe followed him to his grave: the Kings of England, Norway, Spain, Portugal, Belgium, Sweden and Denmark, the Tsar of Bulgaria and the Emperor of Germany. In addition, there were five heirs-apparent (including the ill-fated Archduke Franz Ferdinand of Austria*), seven Queens and a host of minor royalty and foreign ambassadors, representing more than seventy different countries.

> He had succeeded in his kingly profession,
> and he had the instinct of Peace.
>
> (Wilfred Scawen Blunt)

GEORGE V

Born 3 June 1865. Ascended throne 1910. Reigned 25 years.
Second son of Edward VII.
Married Princess Mary of Teck (1893).
Five sons, one daughter.
Died 20 January 1936, aged 70. Buried at Windsor.

The new king was the second son of Edward VII. Without expectation of succeeding to the throne, he was educated as a professional naval officer and saw service throughout the world. The death of his elder brother, the Duke of Clarence, in 1892, forced him to relinquish

* See section on World War I, page 150.

his active naval career and assume the duties of heir-apparent.

In 1893, the Duke of York, as he now was, married his cousin, Princess Mary of Teck (1867–1953). The Princess, better known at this time as Princess May, was the daughter of Francis, Duke of Teck, a minor penurious German Prince, and Mary Adelaide, the daughter of the Duke of Cambridge, seventh son of George III.

George V succeeded to the throne in the middle of a constitutional crisis. The Lords, containing a preponderance of Tory peers, had rejected the Liberal Budget of 1909, the 'Peoples' Budget. This was an unprecedented act and the Liberals were seeking to restrict the powers of the Lords by Act of Parliament. After two elections in 1910 (the only year this has occurred in English history), George V was induced to agree to create sufficient Liberal peers to ensure the passage of the Parliament Bill in the House of Lords, should it be necessary. It became law in August 1911 : the absolute veto of the Lords was reduced to a suspensory veto for two years, and the duration of Parliaments was reduced from seven (1716) to five years.

The First World War broke out in 1914, during which the King made several visits to the front line in France and Belgium. He was a war-casualty himself : during a visit to France in 1915, his horse rolled on him and he received serious internal injuries from which he never fully recovered. The 1914–1918 war enabled the King and Queen to come into close contact with the mass of their people, to an extent unknown since the seventeenth century.

When the war ended the King was fifty-three, with another seventeen years of his reign left and innumerable crises and problems to overcome. The post-war years saw much social unrest and trouble with Ireland.

The 'Sinn Fein' ('Ourselves Alone') Easter Rising of 1916 was followed by the establishment of an independent Parliament in Dublin in 1918. Conferences between Lloyd George and Irish leaders produced the modern partition of Ireland along religious lines, in the Government of Ireland Act, 1920. In 1921 the King and Queen visited Belfast to inaugurate the Northern Ireland Parliament.

Social and industrial unrest resulted in the formation of the first Socialist government, which held office for a brief period, although in a minority in the Commons, in 1924. The Prime Minister was Ramsay Macdonald. In 1926, the 'General Strike' took place : a sympathetic strike by the transport trade unions, in support of the Miners' Federation. The strike lasted from 4 to 13 May, caused the loss of about 160 million working days and involved over two million employed persons. During the strike broadcast news bulletins, which replaced newspapers, proved the importance that radio was to have. The BBC had been established in 1926.

The world economic crisis of 1929–1931 had a drastic effect on England; there was a phenomenal rise in the number of unemployed and the finances of the country were on the verge of collapse. George V was instrumental in persuading the leaders of the three political parties— Ramsay Macdonald (Labour), Stanley Baldwin (Conservative) and Sir Herbert Samuel (Liberal)—to form a National Coalition Government in August 1931, under the premiership of Macdonald.

Not the least important feature of George V's reign was the change in the relationship between Britain and the other members of the Empire. This grew from a demand for self-government in Canada, Australia, New Zealand and South Africa. Prior to 1914, the foreign policy of the Empire was determined by the British government, but after the war Dominion ministers began to express their determination that the imperial system must undergo a radical change, so as to allow the whole Empire some voice in policies which affected the whole. The principle of Dominion independence was gradually accepted, and it received statutory definition in 1931, when the Statute of Westminster created the British Commonwealth of Nations. The Dominions were now no longer a group of colonies subordinated to England, but a Commonwealth of free nations. Outside the Commonwealth were still the Colonies, as distinct from the Dominions, and India. The latter was accorded a measure of self-government in the Government of India Act, 1935, as the beginning of a transitional period which ended with the granting of India's independence in 1947. George V was, incidentally, the first reigning sovereign to visit India, when he attended a Durbar at Delhi in 1911.

George V and Queen Mary's six children were Prince Edward (Edward VIII); Prince Albert (George VI); Princess Mary, the Princess Royal (died 1965); Prince Henry (the Duke of Gloucester); Prince George (the Duke of Kent, killed in an air-crash, 1942) and Prince John, died 1919.

George V celebrated his Silver Jubilee in May 1935, and died on 20 January 1936. He was succeeded by his eldest son as Edward VIII.

EDWARD VIII

Born 23 June 1894. Ascended throne 20 January 1936. Abdicated 11 December 1936.

Eldest son of George V.

Married Mrs Wallis Simpson (1937).

No issue.

Died 28 May 1972, aged 77. Buried at Windsor.

Edward VIII became King on 20 January 1936, and was to have the shortest reign in the country's history, with the exception of that of his namesake, Edward V.

Before the death of George V, rumours were circulating of an attachment which the Prince of Wales had formed and after his accession as king these grew in volume, particularly in American and Continental newspapers; the British press agreed between themselves to ignore the subject. In the autumn of 1936 came the story that the King intended to marry Mrs Wallis Simpson, an American divorcee.

Mrs Simpson, born Wallis Warfield, was the daughter of a Baltimore family, with old and aristocratic connections in Maryland and Virginia. She had divorced her first husband, Lt Winfield Spencer, of the US navy in 1927, and married in the same year Mr Ernest Simpson, a London stockbroker.

With the news that she was filing a divorce petition, the crisis was at hand. On 27 October 1936 she was granted a decree *nisi*, and it became clear that the King intended to marry her. Constitutionally the King could marry whom he wished; but if he did so against the advice of his Cabinet, and the Cabinet resigned on the issue, there would be a general election into which the Crown would be dragged and the concept of constitutional monarchy irreparably damaged.

There were in theory four courses open to the King. He could marry Mrs Simpson and make her Queen; he could contract a morganatic marriage—that is, neither Mrs Simpson nor any issue of the marriage would share in the royal status or property; he could abdicate and then marry; he could abandon Mrs Simpson.

The national objection to Mrs Simpson was not that she was an American, nor that she was a commoner. Both Edward IV and Henry VIII had married commoners, as had the King's own brother, the future George VI. But Mrs Simpson had divorced two husbands, both of whom were still alive; and although there was a royal precedent for a king's marriage to a divorced person—that of Henry II to Eleanor of Aquitane—the idea was disliked. Marriage to a divorced person would raise in acute form the question of the King's relationship to the established Church, whose official doctrine censured the whole concept of divorce. English law did not recognise any such thing as a morganatic marriage. Edward VIII's choice was, therefore, between the abandonment of his project and abdication.

Relations between the King and Mrs Simpson formed the only topic of conversation throughout the British Isles, despite the plight of two million unemployed, Mosley and the Fascists, the Spanish Civil War and the threat of Hitler on the Continent. It was well said at the time that Hitler might have seized Austria without the British public either knowing or caring.

By the Declaration of Abdication Act, 10 December 1936, Edward VIII renounced his throne and was succeeded by his brother, the Duke of York, as George VI; one of the new King's first acts was to create the ex-King Duke of Windsor.

GEORGE VI

Born 14 December 1895. Ascended throne 1936. Reigned 15 years.

Second son of George V.

Married Lady Elizabeth Bowes-Lyon (1923).

Two daughters.

Died 6 February 1952, aged 56. Buried at Windsor.

The Duke of York had an inauspicious accession; only four kings had succeeded to the throne in the lifetime of their predecessors.* But it was soon apparent that George VI had inherited the steady virtues which had distinguished his father and endeared him to the English people. In addition, he had the unfailing support of his wife, and of his mother, Queen Mary, an outstanding Queen Mother at a critical moment in the history of the British monarchy.

His wife, the Lady Elizabeth Bowes-Lyon, though a direct descendant of the kings of Scotland, was a commoner; George had been the first prince (but not princess) of blood Royal to marry a commoner since the reign of George III.

The new king needed all the support he could get. The prestige of the throne was lower than at any time since the accession of Queen Victoria. The abdication crisis would have figured more prominently in British history had it not so soon been overshadowed by the outbreak of the Second World War. This war enhanced the importance of the throne, as the 1914–1918 war had done in George V's time. When it began, King George VI and Queen Elizabeth were little more than constitutional abstractions; by the time it had finished they were firmly entrenched in the nation's affections.

For the greater part of their reign England was at war; the King and Queen set an example of fortitude, raising morale by visiting troops, munitions factories, docks and bomb-damaged areas, freely showing their concern for people under stress. The King also visited the front line in North Africa and Italy.

After the war the emergency coalition, led by Winston Churchill, was replaced by Britain's third Socialist government under the leadership of Clement Attlee. In

* Henry IV, Edward IV, Richard III, William III.

the period from 1945–1950 the Bank of England, the mines, railways, road transport, gas and electricity, the health services, and iron and steel, were brought to some extent under public ownership, and in many ways a social revolution was effected.

George VI died on 6 February 1952, and was succeeded by his elder daughter as Elizabeth II.

ELIZABETH II

Born 21 April 1926. Ascended throne 1952.
Elder daughter of George VI.
Married Philip Mountbatten, RN, formerly Prince Philip of Schleswig-Holstein-Sonderburg-Glücksburg (1947).
Three sons, one daughter.

Queen Elizabeth II's accession was accompanied by a constitutional innovation. She was proclaimed in each of the self-governing countries of what used to be called the British Empire as Queen of that particular country. The formal abandonment of the principle of the indivisibility of the Crown was confirmed by statute in 1953, and a new description, 'Head of the Commonwealth', was inserted amongst the royal titles to allow for the inclusion of republics like India and Pakistan. A feature of the reign has been the number of independent states which have come into being, and the large number of official visits abroad made by the Queen.

As Princess Elizabeth, she married Lt Philip Mountbatten (see next page) on 20 November 1947. There are four children of the marriage: Prince Charles, born 14 November 1948; Princess Anne, born 15 August 1950; Prince Andrew, born 19 February 1960; and Prince Edward, born 10 March 1964.

Portrait: Luke Fildes

Edward VII

Edward VII and the German Kaiser during the former's visit to Germany in 1909

The funeral procession of Edward VII, May 1910

Portrait: O. H. J. Birley

George V

Edward VIII

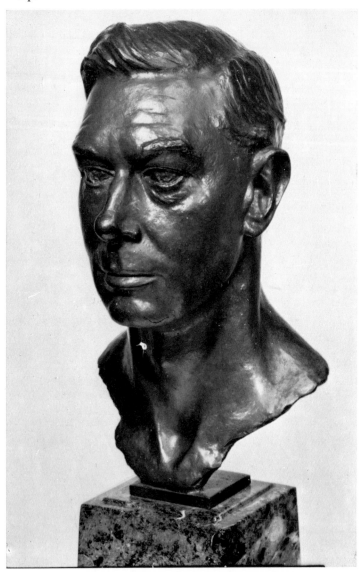

Bust: W. Reid Dick

George VI

Elizabeth, the Queen Mother

Elizabeth II and Prince Philip photographed in the White Drawing Room at Buckingham Palace. The Queen wears the sash and star of the Order of the Garter, with Family Orders on the shoulder; Prince Philip wears the uniform of an Admiral of the Fleet with the sash and star of the Order of the Garter and the star of the Order of the Thistle

The Royal family have of course been affected by the post-war change in social outlook and habits; their frequent travels, at home and abroad, with Prince Philip's cheerful informality and hard work for good causes, have done much to identify them with the everyday life of the nation. At the same time, in an age of recurrent international crises and economic ups and downs, the monarchy's stability and the pageantry still surrounding it have remained a valuable focal point for national self-respect.

In 1965 came the death of Sir Winston Churchill, one of Britain's greatest statesmen; he was given what will probably be the last lavish state funeral. He had served six monarchs and held a variety of high offices from 1905 to 1955, when he retired as Prime Minister, but he will most be remembered for his brilliant leadership in the Second World War.

PRINCE PHILIP, DUKE OF EDINBURGH

Prince Philip was born in Corfu, Greece, on 10 June 1921. He was the fifth child and only son of Princess Alice (a great-granddaughter of Queen Victoria) and Prince Andrew of Greece. Prince Andrew owed his life to George V. In 1922, after Greek disaster in Asia Minor at the hands of the Turks, the Greek ministers in office were executed; Prince Andrew, who had commanded the right wing of the Greek army, was awaiting trial with the certainty of the death sentence following. George V sent an ambassador to Athens and secured his release.

From 1923 to 1935, the Greek Royal family were in exile in England. Prince Philip was educated at Cheam

H

School, Gordonstoun, and Royal Naval College, Dartmouth. During the Second World War he saw active service with the Royal Navy and he served on the battleship *Valiant* at the battle of Cape Matapan (1941).

He became a British subject in February 1947, renouncing his Greek titles, and adopted the name of Mountbatten, the anglicised form of his mother's family name of Battenburg. Before he married Princess Elizabeth, George VI conferred on him the title of Duke of Edinburgh. In 1957, the Duke was granted the titular dignity of Prince of the United Kingdom.

ORDER OF SUCCESSION TO THE THRONE

1. Prince Charles
2. Prince Andrew
3. Prince Edward
4. Princess Anne
5. Master Peter Phillips
6. Princess Margaret
7. Viscount Linley
8. Lady Sarah Armstrong-Jones
9. Duke of Gloucester
10. Earl of Ulster
11. Lady Davina Windsor
12. Duke of Kent
13. Earl of St Andrews
14. Lord Nicholas Windsor
15. Lady Helen Windsor
16. Princess Alexandra
17. James Robert Bruce Ogilvy
18. Miss Marina Victoria Alexandra Ogilvy
19. The Earl of Harewood
20. Viscount Lascelles

INVESTITURE OF THE PRINCE OF WALES

On 1 July 1969, Queen Elizabeth II's eldest son, Charles, was invested as Prince of Wales at a ceremony held at Caernarvon Castle in Wales. He is the twenty-first to hold the title.

MARRIAGE OF PRINCESS ANNE

On 14 November 1973 Princess Anne was married to Capt Mark Phillips. Their son Peter was born on 15 November 1977.

BRITISH WARS AND CAMPAIGNS.
1775–1945

	Date
With U.S.A.	1775–1782
With France	1778–1783
With Spain	1780–1783
With Netherlands	1780–1782
With France	1793–1802
With Napoleon	1803–1815
With U.S.A.	1812–1814
With Russia (Crimean War)	1854–1856
Indian Mutiny	1857–1858
With Abyssinia	1868
With Ashanti	1873–1874
With Afghanistan	1878–1880
With Zulus	1879
With Egypt	1882
With Sudanese	1881–1898
First Boer War	1880–1882
Boxer Rising	1896–1900
Second Boer War	1899–1902
First World War	1914–1918
Second World War	1939–1945

PRIME MINISTERS 1830–1979

1830 Earl Grey	Liberal
1834 Lord Melbourne	Liberal
1834 Sir Robert Peel	Conservative
1835 Lord Melbourne	Liberal
1841 Sir Robert Peel	Conservative
1846 Lord John Russell	Liberal
1852 Earl of Derby	Conservative
1852 Earl of Aberdeen	Lib.-Coalition
1855 Lord Palmerston	Liberal
1865 Earl Russell	Liberal
1866 Earl of Derby	Conservative
1868 Benjamin Disraeli	Conservative
1868 William Gladstone	Liberal
1874 Benjamin Disraeli	Conservative
1880 William Gladstone	Liberal
1885 Marquess of Salisbury	Conservative
1886 William Gladstone	Liberal
1886 Marquess of Salisbury	Cons.-Unionist
1892 William Gladstone	Liberal
1894 Earl of Rosebery	Liberal
1895 Marquess of Salisbury	Cons.-Unionist
1902 A. J. Balfour	Cons.-Unionist
1905 Sir Henry Campbell-Bannerman	Liberal
1908 H. H. Asquith	Liberal
1915 H. H. Asquith	Coalition
1916 D. Lloyd George	Coalition
1922 A. Bonar Law	Conservative
1923 Stanley Baldwin	Conservative
1924 J. Ramsay Macdonald	Labour
1924 Stanley Baldwin	Conservative
1929 J. Ramsay Macdonald	Labour
1931 J. Ramsay Macdonald	National
1935 Stanley Baldwin	National

1937 Neville Chamberlain   National
1940 Winston Churchill   Coalition
1945 C. R. Attlee   Labour
1951 Winston Churchill   Conservative
1955 Sir Anthony Eden   Conservative
1957 Harold Macmillan   Conservative
1963 Sir Alec Douglas-Home   Conservative
1964 Harold Wilson   Labour
1966 Harold Wilson   Labour
1970 Edward Heath   Conservative
1974 Harold Wilson   Labour
1974 Harold Wilson   Labour
1976 James Callaghan   Labour
1979 Margaret Thatcher   Conservative

World War I, 1914-18

BY 1907, Europe was divided into two armed camps:
the Triple Alliance of Germany, Austria and Italy versus
the Triple Entente of Britain, France and Russia. Between 1908 and 1913, a series of events in the Balkans
and North Africa, reflecting nascent nationalism and
international rivalries, brought Europe to the verge of
war.

On 28 June 1914 the heir to the throne of Austria-
Hungary, Archduke Franz Ferdinand, was assassinated
at Sarajevo. Very soon only Italy and England remained
aloof from the general European War. England strove
to confine the war to the Balkans, but after German
violation of Belgian neutrality was brought into the
struggle on 4 August 1914. Italy joined in on the side of
the Allies in 1915.

England's main contribution was on the Western
Front, in France and Belgium. In 1914, and throughout
1915, the BEF, under the command of Sir John French,
stabilised the Allied line southwards from the Channel
ports with very heavy losses, particularly at Ypres and
Loos. At this stage Sir Douglas Haig replaced French.
An attempt to distract attention from the Western Front
by making a landing on the Gallipoli peninsula in the
Dardanelles, was a disastrous and costly failure (1915).
An Allied offensive along the Somme in 1916 gained a
mere seven miles at a cost to England alone of 420,000
casualties.

There were few naval actions. A minor German success at Coronel, off Chile, in 1914 was quickly avenged
at the battle of the Falkland Islands. In May 1916 a

major fleet action took place at the Battle of Jutland. It ended indecisively and was followed by a German submarine offensive against Allied and neutral shipping.

In April 1917 the United States entered the war. This addition of manpower, and the Allied blockade of Germany, meant that the end was in sight. The German High Command withdrew twenty-five miles to the Siegfried, or Hindenburg, line to make Allied offensives more difficult—the Passchendaele offensive (1917) cost 300,000 British lives.

In 1918 the Germans threw all their resources into attacks which seriously undermined their already weak position. From September onwards the German army was on the point of defeat, whilst the civilian population was on the verge of starvation. The Armistice was signed on the morning of 11 November 1918, and ended the war in which three-quarters of a million British soldiers had died.

The peace treaty with Germany was concluded at Versailles (1919). The Allied signatories were Lloyd George (England); Clemenceau (France); Woodrow Wilson (America); and Orlando (Italy). Germany, who had not been a party to the negotiations, was saddled with an astronomical war indemnity, deprived of most of her coal, iron and steel, and separated from her possessions in Eastern Europe. The seeds of World War II were sown by the peacemakers after World War I.

World War II, 1939-45

THE principal cause of the war was Hitler's aggressive and expansionist policy, typified by the seizure of Austria, Czechoslovakia and Poland. England and France declared war on Germany on 3 September 1939, after German entry into Poland on 1 September. The Commonwealth countries followed England's example.

Germany invaded Norway, Denmark, Belgium and Holland; and Russia (bound to Germany in 1939) invaded Finland. The British Expeditionary Force in France found itself cut off and surrounded, and withdrew to Dunkirk, where evacuation took place in May 1940. Italy now entered the war on Germany's behalf; the Germans entered Paris, and England was left alone against the Axis Powers.

In the late summer and autumn of 1940, the Battle of Britain was fought and England saved from invasion. In 1941, Hitler invaded Russia and turned an ally into an enemy. Japan attacked Pearl Harbour and brought the United States into the war, which now became world-wide.

The year 1942 was the turning-point. On land, at sea and in the air, the initiative gradually passed to the Allies. Montgomery and Eisenhower cleared the Germans out of North Africa, the prelude to the invasion of Sicily in 1943. At sea, radar and carrier-based planes were effectively combating the menace of German U-boats. Allied bombing raids ruined the productive capacity of the Ruhr.

The Allied invasion of Sicily in 1943 caused the downfall of Mussolini (July) and led to the Italian Armistice on 3 September. The conquest of German-occupied Italy began. In the Far East (1943), naval battles stemmed the Japanese advance in the Pacific and were followed by American landings on Pacific islands. English and Commonwealth forces halted the Japanese advance in Burma.

Allied landings in Normandy in 1944 resulted in the liberation of France and Belgium. The Allies entered Rome in June 1944. The Russians resumed the offensive on the Eastern Front, in Poland, the Baltic and the Balkans.

In March 1945, the Allies crossed the Rhine. Hitler's death was announced in May, shortly before the Russians entered Berlin. On 9 May the Germans agreed to unconditional surrender. On 12 September, following atom-bomb attacks on Hiroshima and Nagasaki, the Japanese surrendered.

European Monarchy in the Twentieth Century

WHEN Queen Victoria died in 1901, England was one of about twenty European monarchies. In the second half of the twentieth century, only ten remain : Britain (Windsor) ; Denmark and Norway (with the common surname Schleswig-Holstein-Sonderburg-Glücksburg) ; Sweden (Bernadotte) ; Belgium (Saxe-Coburg-Gotha) ; Holland (Orange) ; Luxembourg (Orange) ; Monaco (Grimaldi) ; Liechtenstein (Brandis) ; and Spain (monarchy re-instituted on the death of General Franco in 1975).

Portugal was the first country to lose its dynasty, the Braganzas, in 1910. During and immediately after World War I the Romanovs (Russia), the Hohenzollerns (Germany), the Habsburgs (Austria), and the ruling house of Montenegro were overthrown.

Between the wars Turkey (Ottoman) and Spain (Bourbon) became republics; as did Greece from 1923 to 1935, and again from 1973. The monarchies of Rumania, Yugoslavia, and Bulgaria disappeared during World War II. Italy (Savoy) and Albania became republics in 1946.

THE BRITISH COMMONWEALTH

The member states of the Commonwealth in 1977 are : United Kingdom, Canada, Australia, New Zealand, India, Sri Lanka, Ghana, Malaysia, Cyprus, Nigeria, Sierra Leone, Tanzania, Jamaica, Trinidad & Tobago, Uganda, Western Samoa, Zanzibar, Kenya, Singapore, Malawi, Malta, Zambia, Gambia, Guyana, Botswana,

Lesotho, Barbados, Mauritius, Nauru (special member-
ship), Swaziland, Fiji, Tonga, Bangladesh, Bahamas,
Grenada, Papua, New Guinea.

KINGS AND QUEENS IN EFFIGY

Until the eighteenth century it was the custom when a
great personage died to carry a life-size figure on the
coffin in the funeral procession. Made of wood or wax,
the effigies were dressed as they would have been in life,
and faces in particular were carefully modelled or taken
from a death mask.

Many of these effigies, including some of Kings and
Queens, are still preserved at the Undercroft Museum of
Westminster Abbey, and provide us with excellent like-
nesses.

Among the monarchs represented are :

Charles II, who is dressed in his Garter robes, which
   incidentally are the earliest in England.
Queen Elizabeth. This figure replaces an earlier one,
   and she wears the dress that she wore at the thanks-
   giving service for the defeat of the Spanish Armada.
William III and his Queen, Mary.
Queen Anne, adorned with the star of the Order of
   the Garter.

Other great figures in this collection include William
Pitt, the Duke of Buckingham and Lord Nelson.*

Madam Tussaud's Exhibition in Marylebone Road,
London, has an excellent 'Pageant of Kings and Queens
of England', which includes all the Kings and Queens
from William I to George VI.

* Above information kindly supplied by Lawrence E. Tanner,
CVO, FSA, Librarian, Muniments Room and Library, Westminster Abbey.)

Index